W9-BBF-715

by
Hollis Lee

 VAN NOSTRAND REINHOLD COMPANY
NEW YORK CINCINNATI TORONTO LONDON MELBORNE

Preface

If you own a few acres or plan to acquire a country place, you probably know about the rich rewards associated with country living: the open space, the fresh air, the chance to do some real farming, gardening and animal raising on your own land.

We have published this series of Country Home & Small Farm Guides to provide the basics you'll need to succeed in a broad range of projects and activities on two acres or 100.

We realize that for most people country living is a very private pursuit. After all, a big part of its appeal is not having to look into the next guy's window when you look out of yours. But we hope you will communicate with us. Tell us how you like our books, share bits of country wisdom and suggest additional subjects or services we can provide.

Illustrations by Wayne Kibar

Copyright © 1978 by Van Nostrand Reinhold Company

Library of Congress Catalog Card Number 81-52817

ISBN 0-442-27236-7

Printed in the United States of America

16 15 14 13 12 11 10 9 8 7 6 5 4 3 2

Contents

CATTLE

Raising beef cattle has been an important part of American agriculture since the early Virginia settlements. Large herds of cattle were a familiar sight in the Virginia back country in the 1600s, and on the prairies of Illinois in the early 1800s. Our civilization advanced westward largely because of a vanguard of trappers and miners — and the cattlemen who sought out grasslands where their herds could roam freely without the restrictions of farmers' fences.

Beef consumption has been rising steadily since the end of World War II. One reason is because beef is one of the most nourishing foods available, providing a good source of protein, vitamins and minerals. It offers great variety, ranging from the sumptuous sirloin and T-bone steaks to liver, tongue and heart, which are relatively modest in price. Ground beef is still the favorite; in fact, it would stagger the imagination to envision just how much is consumed in this country in one day. Californians

4

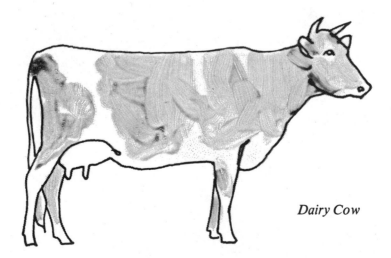

Dairy Cow

alone eat over 2 million pounds a day. If you add to that the consumption in the other 49 states, it obviously would create a mountain of meat. Needless to say, because so much is sold, ground beef is usually a good value.

Beef cattle convert grass into highly palatable, nutritious meat, but to do so, they require large amounts of grass. Most small farms are not large enough to make beef production more than a part-time operation. A cow or two pastured on the small farm will use grass that might otherwise go to waste. Although you may realize a small profit, the primary reason for raising beef animals on the small farm is to provide a good quality meat for home consumption. In addition, *feeding out* the calves makes an excellent project for the younger members of the family who may be involved in 4H or FFA activities.

Beef cattle require care almost every day of the year. You can postpone work in a garden or field for a day or so without severe consequences, but you must maintain a regular schedule in caring for animals. Departure from a schedule will almost surely cause a decline in production; neglect may result in loss of the animals and a sizeable investment.

As more and more families move from urban areas to small farms surrounding our cities, more emphasis will be placed on raising beef animals for home consumption. This book will help you produce enough beef for family consumption, and perhaps, if acreage permits, a few additional head for sale to neighbors or other local outlets.

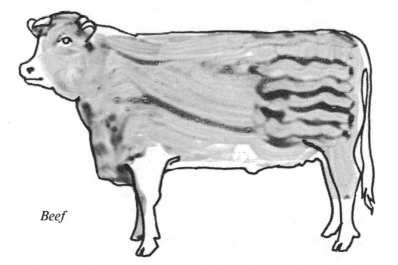

Beef

5

Small Farm Management Systems

You can successfully maintain a small farm beef herd under a wide range of environmental conditions. Beef cattle are now found on small farms far outside of the great western range areas, the traditional home of our beef breeding herds. The southeast part of our country now produces one-fifth, and the far west one-tenth of the nation's total beef production. Beef cattle are being raised on all size farms in all 50 states.

Management of a farm beef herd is complex, and the return on total capital invested in the small farm beef herd may be low. Whether the enterprise is supplementary or full time, net returns will depend on location, cost of land, percentage of cows calving each year, weaning weight, crop yields, and prices received for cattle marketed. The beef herd is best adapted to farms that have an abundance of grasses and *forages* that might not otherwise be used.

There are a number of systems for converting feeds and grasses into beef. These systems break down into two categories: 1) raising a beef breeding herd, and 2) *finishing* purchased beef. Study the following systems for the small farm before you make any decisions.

Systems for Raising a Beef Breeding Herd

Most small acreage farms are not apt to get this involved in the cattle business because of the time requirements and the financial investment. However, if you do decide upon this kind of commitment, choose one of the systems below. Also, read carefully the following section on genetics, essential information for the cattleman who intends to raise and maintain his own herd.

Raising replacements and selling calves

Under this kind of system, the farmer keeps enough *calves* to replace his herd, but sells almost all calves as *feeders* at weaning. The person who purchases the calves raises them for the market.

Selling all calves at weaning

All calves are sold as fat calves for slaughter at *weaning*. This will probably mean *creep feeding* the calves.

Fattening calves for the market

The beef breeding herd is combined with feeding operations. All surplus young cattle are fattened on the farm where produced. Farms best suited for this system have rough, broken, nontillable land that is good for grazing. If the farm also has tillable land from which grain and roughage can be harvested, so much the better.

Another possibility is a combination of grazing and supplemental feeding with *concentrates* to finish the animals for market.

Systems for Finishing Purchased Beef

Under this sort of setup, the cattle raiser purchases feeder cattle and either raises them for market or for another farmer to finish out. One of the following systems is apt to be acceptable to your situation.

Feedlot operation

This system requires no pasture, small amounts of hay or harvested roughage, and large amounts of grain. The cattle are fed in *feed lots* rather on the open range.

Grazing yearlings or calves

The farmer purchases *yearling* or weaning calves and grazes them during the grass season. Later he sells them to a feeder to finish out. The farmer needs large amounts of pasture and hay, but limited grain grazing and feeding.

Grazing and feeding

This operation is a combination of a grazing and a feeding operation, using purchased feeder cattle.

Items to Consider

Now that you have an idea of the options that are open to you, you should consider your own facilities and situation. Some of the following questions should help.

1) What type of farm do you have? Is it suitable for pasture and forage or for growing grain? The most successful operation will be one that provides a maximum utilization of grasses and roughage with a minimum use of grain and feed supplements.
2) How large is your farm?
3) Do markets exist?
4) What is your financial situation? How much can you afford to invest in cattle?
5) Is labor available to help you? Will the cost be small enough for your operation to be successful?
6) Do you have a low enough investment in land that you can keep the cow unit cost at a reasonable level?
7) Do you have the facilities and knowledge to assure raising a large percentage of the calves that are born? Success will also be dependent upon the number of heifers who give birth to healthy calves.

Genetics Primer

If you are going to breed and raise beef cattle, you will find some knowledge of *genetics* helpful, especially if you want to improve your herd. Some of the principles of genetics are outlined here as a basic introduction.

Genes and Chromosomes

The differences among animals result from the hereditary (genetic) differences transmitted by their parents, and the environmental differences in which they are developed. With minor exceptions, each animal receives half of its inheritance from its sire, and half from its dame. The units of inheritance are known as *genes,* which are carried on threadlike material called *chromosomes.* Chromosomes are present in all cells in the body. Cattle have 30 pairs of chromosomes. The chromosomes and genes are paired, each gene being at a particular place on a specific chromosome pair. There are thousands of pairs of genes in each animal, and one member of each pair comes from each parent. All cells in an animal's body have essentially the same makeup of chromosomes and genes.

Special reproductive cells produced in the ovaries of females and the testicles of males contain only one member of each chromosome pair. In this halving process, a sample half of each parent's inheritance goes to each productive cell. The genetic potentialities of a calf are determined at fertilization. The pairing of chromosomes restores the full complement when a reproductive cell from a male fertilizes a reproductive cell from the female. Since half of each of the inheritance traits each reproductive cell contributes is strictly a matter of chance, some reproductive cells will contain more desirable genes for economically important traits than will others.

8   When reproductive cells that contain a high proportion of desirable genes unite, a superior animal results. Sometimes the reproductive cells segregate by chance and recombine upon fertilization. This can cause genetic differences among offspring of the same parents.

A large number of offspring will average the genetic traits of their parents. Some animals will be better, and, on the average, the same number will be inferior. Those that are superior provide the opportunity for herd improvement.

Genes vary greatly in their effects. Some traits are controlled by a single pair of genes, whereas other traits are affected by many. In traits controlled by a single pair of genes, one member of the pair may be dominant. The dominant gene has the capacity for covering up the effect of the other member of the pair. The one covered up is called a recessive gene. For example, the gene for *polled cattle* covers up the gene for horned cattle when both are present. Polled is dominant, and horned is recessive in cattle. Also, the gene for dwarfism is recessive to the gene for normal size in cattle.

Among animals, all differences that are not genetic are classified environmental. Many random environmental factors can affect animals, such as differences in feeding, diseases, injuries and handling, so that these items must be considered in selecting animals.

Genetic Variation

The objective of selecting any performance trait is to increase in the herd the number of desirable genes affecting that trait. This is accomplished by selecting animals that are above average in that trait. *Culling* animals that are poor in a trait reduces the frequency of the undesirable trait if the animals are replaced with ones that are superior in those traits.

Genetic variation is caused by either *additive* or *nonadditive gene effects.* Many genes are involved in the expression of each performance trait. When these genes produce their effects by adding "block upon block," they are referred to as additives. The variations due to additive genes are called *heritability.*

The other basic type of genetic variation is called nonadditive. In this case, the specific combination of genes produces a desirable effect. It is referred to as *hybrid vigor,* or heterosis.

Heritability is the proportion of the differences between animals — measured or observed — that are transmitted to the offspring. The higher the heritability for any trait, the greater the rate of genetic improvement. Traits of economic importance should receive more attention in selecting breeding animals. Make every attempt to see that all environmental factors are as nearly equal as possible. Ignore any traits that have little or no bearing on either efficiency of production or desirability of product.

Methods of Selection

The common methods of selection are as follows: (1) on the basis of pedigree, or performance of ancestors; (2) on the basis of individual performance; and (3) on the basis of performance of progeny. Use all three types of information when you select animals for the breeding stock.

Pedigree
Use pedigree information to select an animal if you don't know anything about its performance or its progeny's performance. Select for items such as longevity, and traits expressed only in one sex, such as mothering or nursing ability.

Own performance
Selection on an animal's own performance will result in most rapid improvement when heritabilities are high. An example of such a trait is growth rate.

Progeny performance
Progeny test information results in the most accurate selection, if the test is adequate. Progeny tests are most useful in selecting for carcass traits and sex-limited traits, such as mothering ability.

Mating Systems
There are five fundamental types of mating systems: (l) random mating, (2) inbreeding, (3) outbreeding, (4) assortative mating, and (5) disassortative mating.

Random mating is mating animals without regard to similarity of pedigree or performance.

Inbreeding is mating animals that are more closely related than the average. **Line breeding** is a form of inbreeding.

Outbreeding is mating animals that are less closely related than the average. *Cross-breeding* is a form of outbreeding.

Assortative mating is mating animals that are more alike in performance tratis.

10

Disassortative mating is mating animals that are less alike in performance traits than the average of the herd or group.

Inbreeding and outbreeding refer to relationship and pedigree. Assortative and disassortative mating refer to phenotypic resemblance (likeness in traits).

Inbreeding
Line breeding is a special kind of inbreeding. It is mating so that the relationship to a particular animal is maintained or increased. Inbreeding normally has some adverse effects on most

performance traits, and reduces general vigor. However, if the animal to which a herd is being line bred is one of outstanding merit, the increase in performance as a result of intensifying the genes of outstanding animals may more than offset any decline in performance due to inbreeding.

When inbred and line bred animals are *outcrossed,* the loss of vigor that has accompanied inbreeding is restored. Line breeding and inbreeding make the animals more alike genetically, and thus more uniform. If an undesirable trait is present in the herd, inbreeding tends to bring it "out in the open." However, inbreeding is not the cause, as the undesirable gene responsible was there all the time. Inbreeding is sometimes used to detect undesirable traits.

Herds should be large and have outstanding genetic merit if line breeding is to be used. Outbreeding is recommended for all commercial operations.

Crossbreeding

Crossbreeding is practiced by commercial breeders to achieve *hybrid vigor* (heterosis). Hybrid vigor results from favorable combinations of genes or groups of genes brought about by specific crosses. Using heterosis necessitates a form of outbreeding, because it usually depends on crossing breeds or groups. The phenomenon of hybrid vigor is used extensively in the commercial production of hogs and chickens. More cattle producers are beginning to use crossbreeding in their operations. A systematic crossing program, involving the use of crossbred cows, has shown an increase in the economic importance of hybrid vigor, as well as fertility and mothering ability of these crossbred cows.

Keep breeding records on each animal. Include information about the rate of growth, birth weight and weaning weight, and performance traits, including all traits that contribute to both efficiency of production and desirability of product.

11

Raising the Beef Breeding Herd

On most small farms, beef cattle will be only one of several enterprises. Therefore, you have considerable flexibility in determining the size of your herd. Keeping the bull to service your cows can be an expensive venture. Because a bull can service 25 or 30 cows in a beef herd, the smaller the herd the more per cow it will cost to keep the bull. However, good bulls should be used. To help offset the cost, some small acreage farmers will buy a young bull, usually in the 800 to 900 pound size, and keep him only for a couple of years. By doing this, they can get growth and maturity on the bull while utilizing his services, and then sell him at a profit. If the herd consists of 10 cows or so, the young bull (with a little help) can service them without difficulty.

You may want to consider owning a bull in partnership with a nearby farmer. Partnerships have worked best where the owners operate on different breeding schedules, i.e., one will strive to have calves born in the spring, while the other operates on a fall schedule.

Artificial insemination has proved to be very successful in breeding beef cattle. However, the success or failure of this method will depend on how closely the cows are observed. In small herds, observing a cow as she comes into heat is relatively easy, but in large herds this will be more difficult as too many may be missed as they come into heat.

The beef herd profits depend largely on the percentage of cows that produce calves each year. Good management strives to achieve as close to a 100% *calf crop* as possible, with a 90% crop considered a reasonable average. It takes a lot of feed and pasture to care for a cow that fails to calve. Unless that cow has some outstanding merits, it will usually pay to market her.

Weaning weights will vary with the type of cattle, the breeding schedule, the pastures and feeding program; however, with good management, it should be possible to obtain an average weaning weight at 7 to 8 months of 500 pounds per calf.

Selecting the Breeding Stock

Any of the leading breeds are well adapted to the small farm, so base your selection on preference. If you stay with one of the local breeds, you will find it easier to find replacements and offer better selections. The market is also usually a little better where there are more animals alike. This is especially true where calves are raised for sale to feeders.

Crossbreeding has increased in practice in the past few years. The crossbred calves tend to be more vigorous and weigh a little more when weaned. Some have performed better in the feed lots as well. However, crossbreeding does not take the place of having good animals with which to build a herd. Good quality is needed in the breeds that are used for the crossbreeding to take advantage of the hybrid vigor. Crossbreeding techniques should be studied if this method of breeding is to be used. In some areas crossbreeding serves additional purposes, as in the Gulf Coast states where crosses between the English-type cattle and the Brahman breeds exhibit greater ability to produce in the hot, humid climate, and are better able to withstand the insects. They show outstanding mothering ability, and produce carcasses equal or only slightly inferior to those from the English breeds.

Bull selection

In selecting the breeding stock for a herd, remember that the bull selection is most important. Regardless of the breed chosen, consider the following characteristics carefully:

1. He should be from a sire and dame with good fertility records.

2. He should have been raised by his own mother and should have weighed more than 500 pounds at weaning.

3. He should have exhibited good gaining ability after weaning, and should weigh 800 to 950 pounds at 12 to 14 months of age.

4. He should be heavy muscled and of accepted breed characteristics, and he should have a skeletal size that will enable him to produce offspring that can be finished to market weight of 1000 to 1150 pounds.

5. He should be disease free. Never buy a diseased animal and try to cure it. The risks are too great to make it worthwhile.

Cow selection

Use the same set of standards to select females as you do to select bulls, although it usually is harder to be as selective. Always strive to get the best quality cows available. The small acreage farmer, having such a small number in his beef herd, needs to get the utmost from each cow. It requires very little more care, feed, grass and hay to raise a superior calf than it does to raise a poor one. Don't waste time and resources on a poor producer.

Cull the cow herd on the basis of regularity of calving, weight, and quality of calves produced. If a cow's first calf is poor, her later calves will most likely also be below par. Cows can be culled effectively in the lower 10 to 25 per cent of a herd on the basis of performance records of one or two of their calves. A cow that does not calve should, of course, be eliminated from the herd.

Conformation Selection

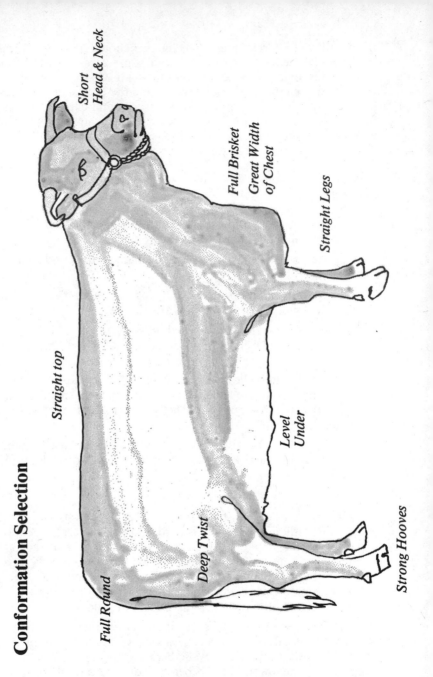

Short
Head & Neck

Full Brisket
Great Width
of Chest

Straight Legs

Straight top

Level
Under

Full Round

Deep Twist

Strong Hooves

Common Faults

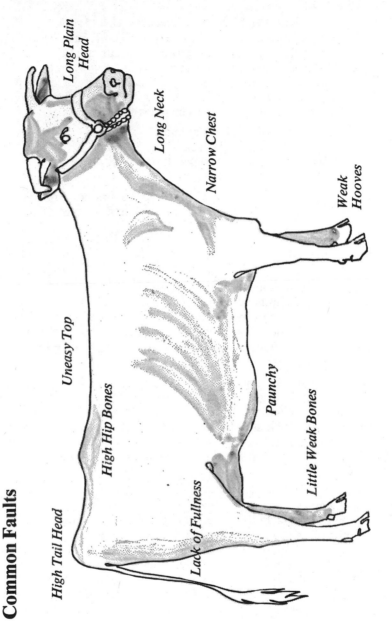

Long Plain Head

Long Neck

Narrow Chest

Weak Hooves

Uneasy Top

High Hip Bones

Paunchy

Little Weak Bones

High Tail Head

Lack of Fullness

15

Raising Replacements for the Herd

If you want to raise your own replacements, save 20 to 40 per cent of the heifers if you want to properly maintain herd numbers. Select heifers that are heavily muscled, with heavy weaning weights and a good rate of gain. Keep performance records to help cull older animals and to select suitable replacements. These records need not be fancy, but be sure to include the following:

1. Identification of each animal.
2. The parentage of each calf.
3. The birth weight of each calf.
4. Weight at or near weaning time.

Cull cows on the basis of health and soundness, fertility and milk production as determined by calf weight at weaning.

Raising heifers

Good pasture is the best and usually the cheapest feed for developing replacement heifers following weaning. Heifers are usually weaned in the fall, and must be fed supplements throughout the winter. The feeding through the first winter should be high enough for the heifers to weigh 600 pounds by the time they reach breeding age, usually 14 to 16 months. This will have the heifers calving at two years of age.

A ration that supports the necessary 1- to 1½-pounds-per-day gain would be 12 to 15 pounds of hay, 3 to 5 pounds of grain and 1 pound of protein supplement. You will not need to supplement legume hay, such as alfalfa or clover. If you have permanent pasture with *frost-cured grass,* you can reduce the hay requirements.

Raising bulls

16

Feed young bulls rather liberally from weaning to 12 to 14 months of age to promote rapid development and earlier breeding use. Liberal feeding will give the young bull an opportunity to show his inherent ability to gain, fatten and develop to normal size. A young bull makes more rapid gains than a heifer; consequently, he will require more feed. Normally he will eat one quarter more feed than the same age heifer. Too much fat on the bull wastes feed and money, and may result in poor fertility.

During the grazing season, good pasture will provide most of the bull's nutritional needs; however, young bulls may need a small amount of supplemental feed. Frequently, some grain is fed 30 to

60 days before and during the breeding season to improve breeding performance. One pound of protein supplement and 5 pounds of grain daily should be ample. The condition of the bull could alter the amount he is fed.

Do not allow the bull to run with the cows the entire year. If it is possible, have a small separate pasture where he can be kept alone during the nonbreeding season. You can let the bull run in the same pasture with pregnant cows and steers, but keep him away from young developing heifers. Most problems with heifers are caused by letting them breed too young. A bull that is healthy and in good breeding condition can be temperamental, so always be cautious and treat him with respect.

Selling Farm-Raised Calves

There has been a big increase in marketing fat calves to individuals who then have the calf custom butchered. Small acreage farmers are taking advantage of this trend by fattening more of the calves they raise. The system they follow may either be immediate full-feeding on high concentrate rations or an increasingly popular system of wintering the calves on a moderately nutritional level the first winter, then grazing them a full season on pasture and full-feeding the animals for 60 to 100 days before slaughter. This permits marketing a heavier animal of approximately 1000 pounds at 18 to 20 months of age that will grade in the high-good to choice range. Heifers handled the same way are usually marketed a little earlier than the steers, since the heifers fatten more rapidly. Either system will work fine for the calves the small acreage farmer raises for home consumption.

Diseases

The beef cattle herd is subject to various diseases and parasites. Animals that receive good care and a well-balanced diet are not as likely to succumb to disease. Good management consists, in part, of insect and parasite control. Follow good sanitary practices, including the elimination of breeding spots for flies, ticks, mosquitoes and other insects. Several cattle diseases are transmitted by these insects. If an animal in the beef herd becomes sick, remove it from the rest of the herd. Consult a veterinarian when your animals are sick.

Feeding the Beef Breeding Herd

In feeding and caring for cows in the beef herd, there is a feeding level that is just the right amount; however, this amount changes from day to day and from cow to cow. With experience, you should be able to determine if the animals are being fed correctly.

The nutritional level should be adequate to maintain the cow in good flesh. Feeding above this level will increase expense without a commensurate increase in production. In addition, keeping cows too fat will increase calving difficulties and calf losses, and decrease milk flow. On the other hand, limiting feed quality and quantity will reduce productivity. It is better to overfeed a little than to underfeed. The saying that you can't starve a profit out of an animal is particularly true with regard to the beef cow.

Feed requirements

The feed required to maintain the cow is roughly proportional to her weight. She needs about 2 pounds of dry matter daily per 100 pounds of live weight to maintain her weight. Much of this can be low quality feed such as hay, grass, cottonseed hulls and similar material. In fact, beef cows must be fed as much low-cost roughage and by-product feed as possible for your beef enterprise to be successful. Fortunately, pasture and grasses are the natural feed for the beef cattle's digestive system.

Although it is a good idea to add a succulent feed to a cow's ration, it isn't necessary, especially during the grazing season. Corn sorghum and various grass silages are excellent additions, but very few small acreage farmers are going to be in a position to have silos and the equipment necessary for making *silage*. Instead, include 5 pounds of good green-colored hay in the cow's ration to meet her daily requirements of Vitamin A. You might want to add a pound or two of protein supplement to meet the protein requirement. Also, some cattlemen feed dry hay to cows that are on good succulent pasture, particularly in the spring.

The beef herd will need to be supplied with minerals. Supply loose or block salt at all times. On the average, cattle will consume about 2 pounds of salt per head per month with less for calves and more for steers on full feed. Requirements for other minerals vary with location. Check with the local county agent for recommendations for your particular location. Iodine, cobalt, copper, iron, and possibly other trace elements are sometimes deficient in local areas.

18

Mineral mixtures that will meet all local requirements are usually available at your local feed dealer.

Beef cattle require an abundance of good, clean, fresh water at all times if they are to produce at their maximum potential.

Winter feeding

Start winter feeding when pasture conditions demand it, not on a specific calendar date. If the cows start to lose weight, start feeding a small amount and increase as necessary. Feed the poorest hay and roughage first and save the best for late winter and calving season. Where possible, feed on the pasture sod. It will reduce cleanup and manure hauling in the spring. If the pasture accumulates a large number of manure piles, run over the pasture with a harrow or disc to break up the piles and scatter them.

Except in the Gulf Coast states, most of the perennial summer pasture grasses used for permanent pastures are dormant and have low nutritional value during the winter. In the south, most of the areas can produce winter grazing with oats, rye, rye grass, wheat, and mixtures that include clovers and vetch. These crops, properly fertilized, will produce winter grazing during a good part of the season. It is more economical to graze temporary winter pasture only 2 or 3 hours a day, and feed hay or roughage for the remainder of the daily ration. Cows will fatten excessively if allowed to graze full-time on good temporary winter pasture.

Cows that calve in the fall and nurse calves through the winter will require more feed to support the milk flow. Add 3 to 5 pounds of 16% protein concentrate feed to their ration. Cows that calve in late winter before spring pasture is available should be fed more liberally as soon as their calves are large enough to benefit from an increased milk flow.

If calves are weaned in the fall, it may be possible to maintain the beef-cow herd well into the winter on frost cured pasture or meadows, or on stalk fields after harvest. The cows can get most of their roughage from such material and this is feed that might otherwise be wasted. Since this roughage is high in fiber and low in protein, it may be necessary to feed about a pound a day per cow of protein supplement, such as cottonseed meal or soybean meal.

One last word of advice — if possible, divide the animals into like groups to feed them. Separate the cows from the calves and yearlings. If you have a timid cow, feed her alone, and if you have an extremely "bossy" cow in the herd, it is better to feed her separately.

Breeding Your Herd

Breeding and raising your own herd can be an economically sound decision. The following information will help you be successful in this venture.

The Breeding Season

If you are a small acreage farmer with a small herd, you will get better results if you limit your breeding season to 2 or 3 months. By doing so, you can choose the most favorable season for calving in your area. Since the calves will be more nearly the same age, you can follow more uniform and systematic management practices.

Systematic calving during two seasons a year may be desirable with a larger herd. This may increase calving slightly since cows failing to settle in one season can be bred the next. Heifers can be bred to calve at 2½ years instead of 2 or 3 years of age.

Most beef calves are dropped in late winter or early spring. They should arrive 3 to 6 weeks before spring growth starts on the grass. As the grass begins to grow, they will be large enough to utilize the increased milk flow from the cows. Because you will probably need to wean the calves in the fall when the grasses become dormant, those born early in the spring will develop into heavier, more valuable calves at weaning.

In the deep south and far west, some herds have breeding seasons to drop fall calves. They rely on winter type grasses such as fescue, clover, rye grass, oats, wheat, and other small grains. This type of pasture can be better utilized by yearlings and 2-year-olds to produce meat. In the north, fall calves seldom do as well as calves born in the spring.

Breeding Heifers

Heifers are cows that have never had a calf and are less than three years old.

On the small farm, heifers should be bred to calve at two years old. This procedure is encouraged (1) if the heifer grows rapidly and weighs 600 pounds or more at breeding, and (2) if experienced help can be available at calving time to give special attention to the heifers.

Research has shown that heifers bred to calve first as 2-year-olds will raise 0.7 more calves during their lives than heifers bred to calve first as three-year-olds. The early breeding has little, if any, effect on size of the heifer at maturity, and apparently does not reduce length of productive life. Heifers calving as 2-year-olds often require help, and calf losses may be higher than average. Since crossbreeding calves show a higher rate of survival, cross-breeding of heifers might be considered for first calving. Younger bulls may also help.

Heifers should be bred at a different time than the older cows so that they can get more attention at calving time. Heifers that calve just before or during early spring receive the full benefit of succulent green grass to increase their milk flow. Otherwise, the heifers will need extra feed after calving to support continued growth during lactation. Cows will breed easier if they are gaining weight.

Giving Birth

Gestation

The *gestation period* for a cow is about 283 days, or about 9½ months. A variation of 10 days either way from the average is not unusual. As the cow's time for calving approaches, the udder becomes distended with milk, and there is a marked "loosening" or falling away in the region of the tailhead and *pin bones*. The *vulva* swells and enlarges considerably.

Calving

Watch cows closely at calving time. When cows calve during the grazing season, leave them in a small pasture near the house and check on them twice a day. A clean pasture is better than a barn, primarily because there is less chance of infection and injury. If a cow is expected to calve during severe weather, she should be put in a clean stall.

Normally, most cows will calve without assistance, but be alert for signs of trouble. Either assist or call a veterinarian if, after two hours of severe labor, she has not calved. Be especially alert with young heifers having their first calves.

Once the calf is born, if it does not begin breathing immediately, wipe away any mucus from its mouth or nostrils, and induce natural breathing by alternate compression and relaxation of the walls of the chest. Protect the calf in cold weather, and keep it warm until it is dry and on its feet. Once it gets on its feet, it will start nursing.

Even though a cow may have more milk than the calf can take the first few days, she will quickly adjust her milk output to a level the calf can take. Failure to remove excess milk does not increase the frequency of spoiled udders. Be sure that the calf nurses all of the teats and does not leave one, as this can cause a problem.

21

Raising the Calves

Weaning

To wean calves that have been running with the cows in the pasture, confine them in a pen or barn out of sight and hearing of the cows. (This will be almost impossible on most small farms.) Offer the calves some good hay, and a little grain during this period of two to three weeks. The cows will be dried off by this time. The pressure that builds up in the udder will stop further secretion of milk, so do not milk her after the calf has been removed.

Creep feeding

Creep feeding calves with concentrates will often pay good dividends when the calves are to be marketed for slaughter at or soon after weaning. The creep feed, in addition to putting extra weight on the calves, also increases the grade at which they can be marketed. During drought or grass shortage, creep feeding the calves keeps them growing and holds their finish. It also helps to reduce the drain on the cows. Creep feeding ordinarily is not economical if the calves are to be carried over the winter and grazed the next season.

Dehorning

Calves in a commercial beef herd should be dehorned if they are not a polled breed. This can be done most easily before the calves are 3 weeks old, when the tender horn "buttons" first appear. Scrape them with a knife to irritate the surfaces, then carefully apply the moistened tip of a caustic pencil (stick of potassium hydroxide). The caustic pencil causes a scab to form on the irritated areas. After a few days the scab will shrivel and fall off, leaving a hornless or polled calf. Commercial liquids and pastes are also available to use for dehorning. Electrically heated irons are sometimes used by applying the heated tip to the base of the horn button. Large calves whose horns have already started to grow can be dehorned with a dehorning tool that looks something like a bolt cutter.

22

Castrating

Male calves must be castrated to produce beef that meets market demands. The castration should be done before the calf is 3 or 4 months old, but they are a lot less trouble if they are castrated within the first few days after birth. They bleed less, and there is less danger of infection. Heifers are seldom spayed on farms. Tests have shown that spayed heifers actually make slower gains.

The U. S. Department of Agriculture has an excellent bulletin, No. 2141, that provides information on "Dehorning, Castrating, Branding, and Marking."

Finishing Purchased Beef Cattle

Some small acreage farmers prefer to buy feeder cattle and raise them for the market rather than breed their own herds.

Types of Feeder Cattle

Feeder cattle range from 350 pound calves to older feeders weighing 1,000 pounds. They are available for purchase in large numbers in the fall, at the end of the grazing season, with peak numbers in October. Some feeders are available almost any day of the year. Don't try to outguess the market. Buy when you are ready and need the feeders. Important characteristics of the more common ages and weights are described below.

Calves

A calf is a cow that is less than one year old. Some of the advantages and disadvantages of purchasing calves are listed below.

1. They make more efficient gains than older cattle.
2. They make possible maximum flexibility by being adaptable to many different systems of cattle feeding.
3. They require longer feeding or grazing periods to reach popular market weights.
4. They use relatively less roughage and more grain than older animals if fed out directly for slaughter.
5. They require high-quality feeds; thus, calves are not well adapted to cleaning corn fields or making use of low-quality roughage, pasture, or feeds.
6. They are likely to have more sickness and higher death losses.
7. They are lighter at purchase; therefore, a high proportion of the weight sold is gain. Efficiency of feeding is more important in feeding calves.

23

Yearlings

A *yearling* is a cow in its second year of growth. Some of their advantages and disadvantages are listed below.

1. They tend to have fewer health problems than younger cattle.
2. They go on feed and finish faster than calves.
3. They allow more flexibility in feeding programs without getting too heavy for market demands.
4. They can use relatively large amounts of roughage, some of which can be low quality.

Grades of Feeder Cattle

Feeder cattle range from well-bred beef animals to nondescript or dairy-bred cattle. Grades are Prime, Choice, Good, Standard and Utility. Consider the following when deciding what quality or grade to feed:

1. The animals should be healthy.
2. Ordinarily, cattle of a given feeder grade can be profitably finished only to the corresponding slaughter grade or one grade higher; that is, Good feeders should be finished to Good or Choice slaughter grades, but not higher.
3. Lower grades are best adapted to high-roughage rations.
4. Lower grade feeders sell relatively low in the fall. Thus, they are best adapted to short winter feeding on a ration of high roughage. Beware of stunted, parasitized, or diseased cattle.

Feeding the Cattle

Getting cattle regulated on fattening feeds is a developed art, and no definite rules applicable to all conditions can be given. Use the suggested rations as a guide only. Quality of feed available, type of grain and protein available, and relative prices will influence the specific ration to be used.

Types of grain

For all practical purposes, you can use corn, barley, or sorghum grain interchangeably, although gains on sorghum and barley may not be quite as efficient. Some feeders say that, using corn as a base of 100, sorghum and barley equal 90 percent. Rolled wheat is an excellent feed when used in the ration for up to 50 percent of the grain. Dried beet pulp, citrus pulp and molasses can all be used as part of the ration, but you will need to adjust the protein level in the ration. The amount of protein supplement needed depends on the type available, and should be determined on the price per pound of digestible protein in the supplement. Cottonseed, soybean, linseed, and peanut meals are the most commonly used and readily available. When fed with conventional rations, there is no appreciable difference between these meals.

Preparing the feed

You may use a variety of methods to prepare suitable feed. Grains in cattle *finishing rations* should be coarsely ground or rolled. The two methods are about equally satisfactory. Steam rolling milo, corn and barley is also satisfactory, but it's more costly. Chopping or coarse grinding hay usually reduces waste, increases consumption somewhat, and may increase gains slightly.

Lower quality roughage usually benefits most from chopping or grinding. Roughage should not be finely ground. Feeding complete, ground, mixed rations is often more convenient, and such rations aid in getting the cattle "on feed."

Pelletizing feed increases gains slightly, plus there is less waste. However, the cost is higher so it is doubtful if pelletizing is economically worthwhile.

When feeding complete mixed rations, take care to insure that they contain adequate protein, carbohydrates, minerals and vitamins. You can provide salt separately, as a free choice, or added to the ration at a level of ½ to 1 percent. During long feeding periods, increase the ration to respond to the increased size of the animals.

Starting the cattle

Cattle can be started on 60 to 70 percent roughage rations. If concentrates and roughages are fed separately, roughage can be self-fed and concentrates increased gradually. The objective is to work up to a desired level rapidly, but if this is done too rapidly, the micro-organisms that inhabit the rumen will not have sufficient time to adjust to the new ration, and the cattle will go "off feed." Different herds of cattle will not react the same.

Increase concentrate percentages until, when on full feed, they are eating 2 pounds or more of grain per day per 100 pounds of body weight. The finishing ration for dry lot 400 to 450 pound calves should consist of an average of 5 pounds of hay, 13 pounds of grain, and 1¼ pounds of 41% protein supplement over a 275 day feeding period. On this ration, the steer should gain an average 2 pounds per day, and weigh from 950 to 1000 pounds at the end of the finishing period. Heifers will require one pound less of grain per day and one pound less of hay, on the average. Their feeding period normally will require approximately 225 days.

Deferred feeding system

25

If you use the deferred feeding system, pasture the steers for 120 days with enough roughage and protein concentrate to produce an average gain of 1½ pounds per day. Then start them on a daily finishing ration of 7 pounds of hay, 15 pounds of grain and 1 pound of protein supplement. On the average, this should produce a 2 to 2½ pound daily gain over a period of 60 to 100 days.

Balancing the ration

The foregoing discussion has necessarily involved some approximates and the application of "rule of thumb." The idea is to have a balanced ration that meets the requirements for a specific animal at his specific weight. Morrison's handbook on Feeds and Feeding is an excellent source for detailed information.

Balancing a ration involves finding a combination of feeds that will supply the required nutrients. For example, the daily requirements for a 400 pound calf being fattened in the dry lot would be:

Dry matter	10 pounds
Total protein	1.3 pounds
Digestable protein	1.0 pounds
Total digestible nutrients	8.0 pounds
Calcium	.044 pounds
Phosphorus	.033 pounds
Carotene	25 milligrams
Vitamin A	10,000 U.S.P. units

A daily ration of 10 pounds of corn, 1½ pounds of cottonseed meal, and 4 pounds of hay would provide the nutrients required. The minerals needed would have to be added to complete the ration.

Facilities for Beef and Dairy Cattle

Beef Cattle

You will not need many facilities to raise beef cattle on the small farm unless you purchase feed in large quantities for a dry lot feeding operation.

Shed

Because you will probably raise cattle on a limited scale, your main facility will be an open shed that provides 30 to 40 square feet of space per animal. In the moderate and southern climates the shed should be enclosed on the north and east sides in order to furnish a wind break. In the more northerly areas, the shed may be completely enclosed. If trees or other types of shade are not available, the shed can furnish shade for the cattle; steers will gain up to 1/4 more weight in hot weather if shade is provided.

Corral

A small corral divided into two sections, and having a *cutting chute* equipped with a *head gate,* will be needed. A loading chute for loading and unloading animals is not an absolute necessity, but is very handy. Most small acreage farmers will not be blessed with

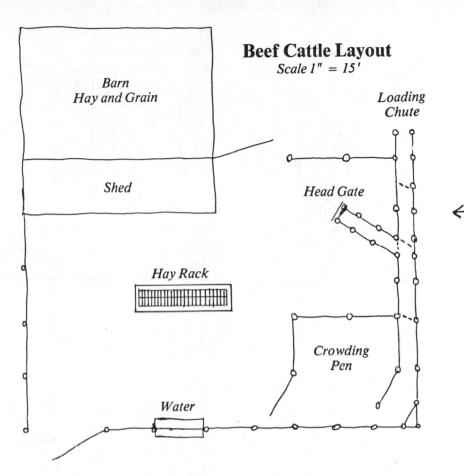

Beef Cattle Layout
Scale 1" = 15'

Barn
Hay and Grain

Loading
Chute

Shed

Head Gate

Hay Rack

Crowding
Pen

Water

very much help, so they should take advantage of all the labor saving devices possible.

Storage

A feed storage area for beef cattle should provide for hay storage, and grain or protein supplement storage. For hay storage, a good rule of thumb guide is 20 lbs. of hay per day for each cow times the normal number of feeding days (20 lbs. of hay x 100 days = 1 ton of hay per cow). Most feeding programs will require that the hay be supplemented with grain and high protein feed, most of which is purchased in sacks or bags. Storage space for this feed should be convenient to the feed troughs, easy to get to for unloading, weathertight and rodent-proof. Small metal bins have proved very satisfactory for grain storage.

28

Loading Chute

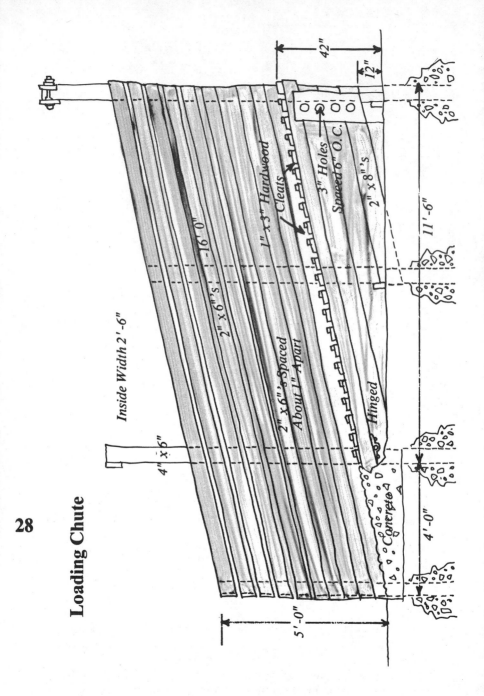

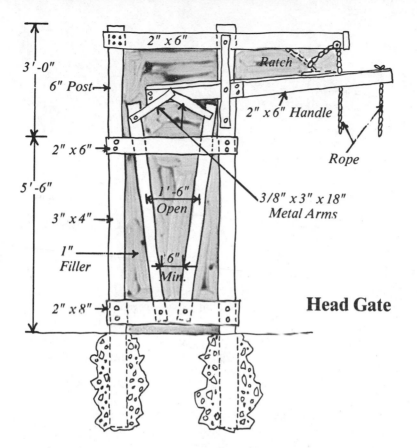

3'-0"

6" Post

2" x 6"

5'-6"

3" x 4"

1"
Filler

2" x 8"

2" x 6"

Ratch

2" x 6" Handle

Rope

1'-6"
Open

3/8" x 3" x 18"
Metal Arms

6"
Min.

Head Gate

Racks and troughs

Hay racks and feed troughs will pay for themselves in a short time by eliminating waste. You will need 36 inches of hay rack and 24 inches of feed trough for each mature animal.

Feeding facilities

Feeding is normally done in one of two ways, the open feed lot system, or confinement housing. Open feed lots consist of open-front buildings with an outside lot for feeding. The lot is preferably paved, and the feeding is done in auger bunks or fence line feeders. The feed is delivered by self-unloading wagons or trucks. In the confinement system the cattle are kept in a building equipped with a ventilation system to help regulate the temperature. Most have slotted floors, manure storage pits, and a liquid manure handling system.

The dry lot system has been conventional in the cattle feeding areas; however, there is a trend to confinement feeding. Open lots

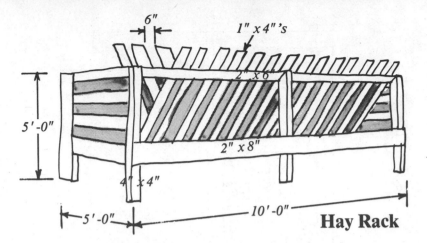

6"

1" x 4"'s

2" x 6"

5'-0"

2" x 8"

4" x 4"

5'-0"

10'-0"

Hay Rack

are the choice of large operations, while confinement appears to be the choice of owner operated farms.

The confinement system, although considerably more expensive to establish does have the following advantages:

1. Surface run-off of waste products may be eliminated to minimize air and water pollution. EPA now requires that feedlots meet established standards. States also have certain requirements.
2. The manure does not lose as much of its value for fertilizer.
3. If properly constructed, it requires less labor to handle the waste products.
4. Feeding can be more easily mechanized.
5. The workers can observe the cattle better and be in a position to correct problems that develop, such as feeding problems and diseases.

Feeding out

The feeding out of beef cattle is not a normal activity for the small acreage farmer, although he may feed out a small number of calves from his own herd, or those purchased elsewhere for that purpose. The facilities for such an operation are basically the same as those required for his regular herd. Just make certain that the facilities are adequate to take care of the number of animals on hand.

Dairy Cattle

Most small acreage farmers will consider keeping one or two milk cows to provide their families with fresh milk, cream and butter. Facilities for a family size operation will be minimal.

Basic facilities

A small barn with a milking stall, feed storage areas and calf pen is about all you will need. The milking stall should be about 5 feet by 8 feet in size, and equipped with a 30-inch long x 24-inch wide x 10-inch deep feed trough, as most milk cows are fed as they are being milked. The hay storage area should be large enough to accommodate a three or four month supply of hay based on a requirement of 30 pounds per cow per day. A small rodent-proof room will be needed to store the grain and protein supplement. The calf pen shelter area should be 8 feet x 10 feet for one calf, with another 4 feet x 5 feet added for each additional calf. The calf pen should be equipped with a creep feeder and a fresh water trough.

These facilities can be as plain or elaborate as you want them, but bear in mind that the ultimate effect of poorly constructed facilities will be more noticeable for the workers than for the animals. Nothing takes the joy out of owning a good milk cow faster than having to milk her outside in a cold, hard rain, or in a poorly constructed shelter that will not keep out the wind, rain or snow. Temperatures between 10° F. and 75° F. do not appreciably affect milk production, but they can affect your attitude because almost 75 per cent of the work performed is in the milking area. A

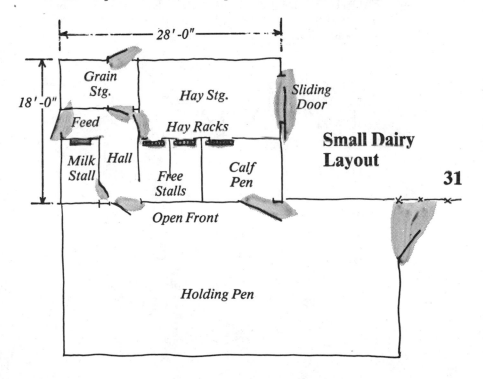

Small Dairy Layout

31

warm, dry milking stall will certainly be appreciated on those cold, rainy or snowy days.

In addition to providing warm, dry stalls for inclement weather, it is also important to provide adequate ventilation during warm weather. Milk production will be depressed during periods of high temperatures, so provide good ventilation for the warm seasons of the year.

Location of facilities

The feed storage areas should be handy and conveniently located with easy access for unloading feeds and hay. Arrange the lots and pens to allow for easy movement of animals to and from the pasture areas, with easy access to water at all times. Barns and pens should also have sufficient accessibility to allow equipment to move about for cleaning. Gates should be a minimum of 10 feet wide, wider where possible. Locate lights and electrical outlets conveniently within the barn.

Free stall area

A free stall area is recommended in the resting area. The cows stay cleaner, and milking time is reduced as less washing time is required. Also, damage to udders and teats is less likely. The recommended free stall size is 4 feet x 8 feet, with floors consisting of dirt, sand or gravel (plus bedding), but not paved, with easy access to hay racks and water.

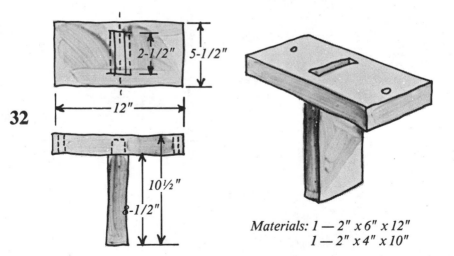

Materials: 1 — 2" x 6" x 12"
1 — 2" x 4" x 10"

Milking Stool

Breeds of Cattle

The Hereford

The Hereford is the leading beef cattle breed in the United States. The Hereford was introduced into this country in the early 1800's. The breed has been favored because it will adapt to a wide range of conditions and produce the finest quality beef.

The Hereford is distinctly a beef breed. Individuals of the breed are rather rectangular in form, deep bodied, thick fleshed, and possess excellent constitution and vigor. The breed has long been noted for its ability to forage over a wide area. The thick coat of hair, robust constitution and easy-keeping quality has made it

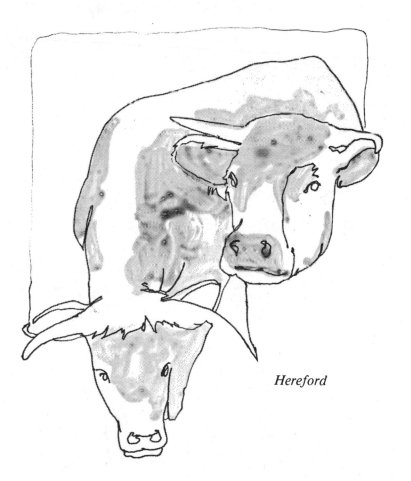

Hereford

unusually well suited to range conditions. Although the cows are not noted as good milkers, they still are able to raise choice calves.

The Hereford color is distinctive. The body is a rich medium red, and the face snow white. The white color is also found on the underline, flank, chest, breast, knees and hocks. In purebred animals, it is also important that the white extend down the neck, commonly called a "feather-neck." The term "white-face" is used to identify the Hereford in cattle country. The white face is a dominant gene in the breed, and in crossbreeding it tends to overshadow others.

Aberdeen-Angus Breed

Aberdeen-Angus cattle are distinguished from other breeds by their jet black color, comparatively smooth coat of hair, and the polled character.

Angus are slightly smaller than most other beef breeds. Because of their compactness and closeness to the ground, they are often underestimated in weight. They are compact, broad, deep, smooth, heavily muscled, and have a cylindrical body. The Angus mature at an early age, are heavily muscled in the region of the high-priced cuts of beef, and yield a high *dressing percentage.*

Aberdeen-Angus have won favor with stockmen who produce their beef on high producing improved pastures. Because of their short stocky build, they are more at home grazing improved pasture than trying to cover large areas of native range land. They are used extensively in crossbreeding programs.

34

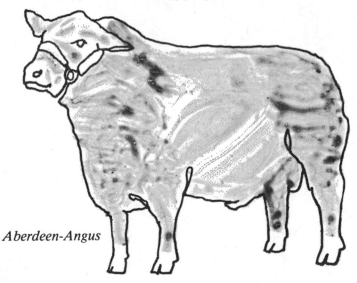

Aberdeen-Angus

Shorthorn Breed

Shorthorn cattle have a long and illustrious history, being one of the oldest of the recognized breeds. The breed appears in a wide range of colors. Roans (red-blended with white hair) are perhaps the most numerous, although Shorthorns may be red, white, or any combination of the two. The nose should be "flesh colored." The Shorthorns are the largest of the standard beef breeds. The large rectangular body and broad back are identified with the Shorthorn.

The Shorthorn has a good, even temperament with good

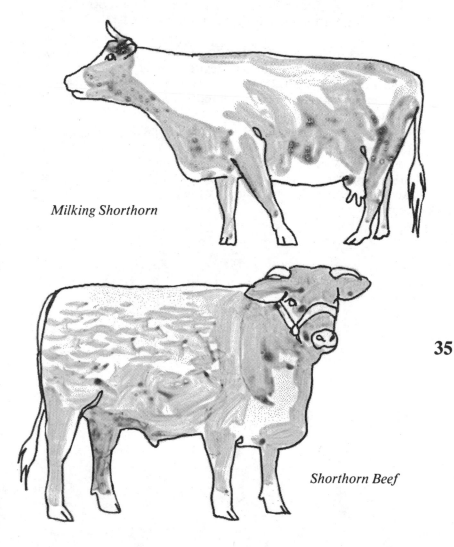

Milking Shorthorn

Shorthorn Beef

grazing ability and excellent milk production. These factors have made the Shorthorn a favorite with small farmers.

One strain of Shorthorns has been developed for its milking ability. The milking Shorthorn has long been a favorite on many farms in the United States. This breed offers the small acreage farmer beef and milk in one animal. The cow can furnish milk for the family, and the calf can be fattened for beef.

There is also a closely related breed of dual-purpose cattle called the Red Poll. As the name indicates, the breed is red in color, and is hornless. There has been so much crossbreeding between the milking Shorthorn and Red Poll that it is hard to separate the two.

The Brahman (Zebu)

The Brahman is not a breed of cattle as such, but rather a type of cattle that is native to India. There are thirty or more breeds of Brahman, and several have been imported into the United States. The Guzerat and Nelloze have been the chief breeds used.

Brahman cattle are characterized by a large hump over the shoulders, an abundance of loose, pendulous skin under the neck, and a narrow and upstanding body with long legs. They also have long, droopy ears and a grunty voice. The Brahman have sweat glands and are, therefore, able to withstand more heat than the

36

Brahman

European breeds. This, and the apparent ability to cope with insects, has made them popular in the South and Gulf Coast areas. They have the ability to rustle for forage and water, and have inherited outstanding mothering instincts.

Several new breeds of beef cattle have been developed using the Brahman crosses. Santa Gertrudis, developed by the King Ranch of Texas, is one of these breeds. Beefmaster is a three way cross using Brahman, Shorthorn and Hereford. Brangus is an Angus and Brahman cross. These strains have shown promise in certain areas of the country. The lack of high fertility seems to be the major problem.

Imported Cattle

Exotic isn't a word normally used to describe cattle, but that's exactly what certain breeds of beef-type cattle are called that are being imported into the United States. They are referred to as "exotic" because they are not common to existing predominantly British-type cattle herds. These imported breeds are from Europe, mostly from Switzerland, France and Italy. Such breeds include Charolais, Limousin, Chianina, Semmental, and Gelbrich.

Importing these breeds on a large scale is quite a problem. Most of the countries they come from are plagued with foot and mouth disease, so that animals must first be transferred to a country that is free of the disease before they can be imported into the United States. This procedure takes about a year, and is very expensive.

Experiments using these exotic breeds in crossbreeding programs have given mixed results. While the calves from such crosses outweigh standard Angus and Hereford calves at weaning, they have higher death rates, grade lower in quality, and prove less tender than standard breeds. Therefore, much testing remains to be done before it is known if the "good" features outweigh the "bad." **37**

SHEEP

As with other classes of livestock, sheep breeders are divided into two categories, (1) commercial producers and (2) purebred breeders. The commercial breeders are primarily concerned with securing a high percentage lamb crop and with utility features of the animals, including their ability to make efficient use of available feeds. Sheep have economic potential because they require a low capital investment and because they are a short-term stock — 8 months after the ewe is bred, there is a product to market. The purebred breeders are interested in producing rams for sale to commercial sheepmen. The small acreage farmer should concentrate on a commercial operation until he feels equipped to handle the complexities of the purebred breeder-type operation.

Successful sheep production on the small farm depends upon maintaining a healthy and highly productive flock that is well managed, and upon marketing the lamb and wool crop. The farm

flock method of production is the common system used on small farms. This method stresses market lamb production, with wool production of secondary importance. Most of the sheep in farm flocks are of the *mutton type.*

During the grazing season, the sheep usually compete with other classes of livestock for use of permanent or seeded pasture. On too many farms, sheep are considered scavengers, and are given the assignment of keeping down weeds and grasses along fence rows, lanes and poor grazing areas. It is true that sheep can graze lands unsuited for cattle, and can use leftovers such as beet tops and fallen corn which can be converted into choice lamb. However, sheep are more efficient forage converters than cattle, and should be entitled to their rightful share of the good pastures. Good pastures, and a system of pasture rotation, are two of the management tools that help to insure profitable operations.

Regardless of the location of your country place, year-round grazing is desired, and sheep can utilize the various grasses, legumes, weeds, herbs and shrubs that grow in different locations, and that grow during the different seasons as well.

Abundant and succulent pastures are ideal for stimulating milk production in ewes. Moreover, pastures of this type are desirable for the young lamb, which has a limited digestive capacity. Accordingly, the degree of *finish* carried by lambs at market time is an accurate reflection of the amount and quality of the forage available on the pasture.

Good pastures allow for intensive management of sheep, ease land pressure by requiring less land, reduce labor needs, require less feeding, and increase the number of lambs raised, percentage-wise.

Establishing the Flock

If you intend to keep sheep for both market lambs and wool, select individual lambs whose characteristics will insure maximum and efficient production of these two products. In addition, if you want to make progress in the breeding program, each succeeding generation must represent an improvement over the parent stock.

Establishing a flock of sheep is not unlike establishing a herd of cattle, hogs, or horses. Sheep can be more confusing because two major products are involved, lambs and wool, and because there are more breeds to choose from. Unless the price of purebreds is unusually favorable, start with crossbred or grade *ewes,* and a purebred ram.

Selecting the Breed

In starting a farm flock, the question often arises as to whether native or western *ewes* should be purchased. Western ewes are produced in the range areas, and they have a predominance of fine-wool breeding. They are more uniform, smaller and less costly. The so-called native ewes produced outside of the range areas are primarily of the mutton-type breeding. They are larger, and they produce a larger lamb. Both types are found throughout the country. The owner's preference is usually the deciding factor since there is very little difference in special-area adaptations of different breeds. In the west, the fine-wool breeding is used chiefly because of the herding instincts of the animals.

Two breeds have been developed by the U. S. Department of Agriculture, Agricultural Research Service at Dubois, Idaho. One is the larger Columbia, for the lush ranges of the west, and the smaller Targhee for average ranges.

If you want out-of-season lamb production, purchase ewes of the Dorset, Tunis, Rambouillet or Merino breeding because they are about the only ones that consistently breed at times other than late summer and early fall.

Size of the Flock

The size of the flock on the small farm will no doubt be determined by how much land is available, and how well the pasture is improved. However, labor and equipment costs, except at lambing time, differ very little whether the flock numbers 12 or 50. The smaller flock will require the services of one ram, and practically the same amount of fencing to provide rotation of pastures and suitable corrals for protection from dogs.

Purchasing the Flock

Late summer, after the lambs are weaned, is the best time to purchase ewes to start a flock. At this time of the year, you can buy some of the surplus ewes from neighboring farms, or obtain a selection of ewes from terminal markets. Ewes can usually be purchased at reasonable prices at this time, and for beginners there is a period of valuable training prior to lambing time. When purchasing, make certain that the ewes are not culls (shy breeders and ewes with unsound udders or other defects) from one or several flocks. From this standpoint, the purchase of yearlings affords the best protection.

Most established sheepmen select yearling ewes for their flock that will be bred to lamb as two year olds. However, if you are a novice, begin the flock with older ewes until you gain experience necessary to handle the young ewes.

When you are purchasing sheep, pay attention to their physical condition. Select ewes that are in good, thrifty, vigorous condition. They should give evidence of being capable of producing a good fleece and raising strong, healthy lambs. Do not purchase animals that have a dark blue skin, paleness or lack of coloring in the lining of the nose and eyelids, listlessness or lack of vigor, and a general rundown appearance.

Select *ewes* with the primary objective of wool production and fat lamb production. It will be almost impossible to select by production testing, or on the basis of pedigree. Therefore, use a mental picture of the ideal, and select for plenty of size, good width, depth, and compactness of body; a short, wide head with large, clear eyes; a short, thick neck; a wide, deep chest; good spring of rib; lowness in both fore and rear flank; a wide, strong back; width and thickness through the loin; length and levelness over the rump; a large leg of mutton; plenty of bone; straight legs and closeness to the ground; a fleece of acceptable weight and quality, and a pink skin. No animal is perfect; therefore, the bad points must be weighed against the good in making selections.

The sketches show the ideal type with its good points, and the common faults to avoid where possible.

Determining Age

The age of sheep can be determined fairly accurately by their teeth. Lambs up to about 14 months have small narrow milk front teeth in the lower jaw. At this age, the two center incisor teeth in the lower jaw are replaced with 1 pair of permanent broad teeth. Each succeeding year, an additional pair of permanent teeth appear, one on each side of the first pair, until at age four there is a full mouth. After four years, it is impossible to determine the exact age. As time goes by, the teeth will wear and spread apart. Often, some are lost after about the fifth or sixth year resulting in what is called a "broken mouth" ewe.

41

Handling Sheep

Sheep should be caught around the neck, by the hind leg, or by the rear flank. They should never be caught by the wool. Such treatment will injure the skin and tissue. Keep your fingers together when handling sheep. To observe the fleece and skin, part the wool on the shoulder or side. Opening the fleece on the back will allow water to enter.

Mutton Type
Selection Points

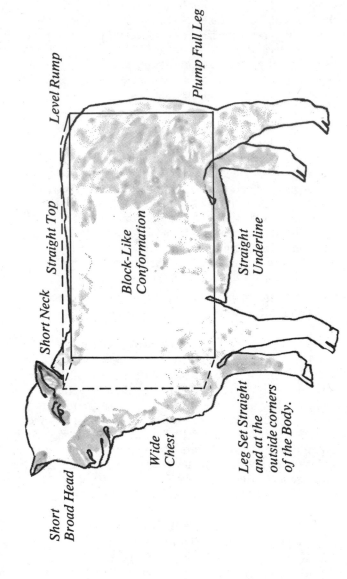

Level Rump

Plump Full Leg

Straight Top

Short Neck

Block-Like Conformation

Straight Underline

Short Broad Head

Wide Chest

Leg Set Straight and at the outside corners of the Body.

Conformation Faults

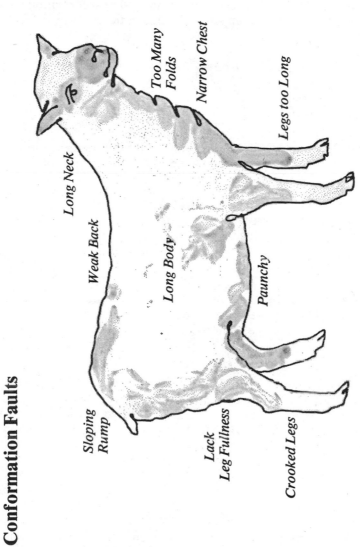

Long Neck

Weak Back

Sloping Rump

Long Body

Lack Leg Fullness

Paunchy

Crooked Legs

Too Many Folds

Narrow Chest

Legs too Long

43

Breeding

Sheep were probably the first animal domesticated by man. As a result, there is much scientific information available about their breeding habits. Even so, not all of the phenomena are clear, and much work still remains to be done. The information that follows should help you understand some of the breeding habits of sheep.

Puberty of Sheep

The ram lamb's sex organs become functional at 4 to 7 months. The ram lamb will sometimes breed a few ewes prior to his normal weaning age.

The ewe lambs are a little slower in reaching sexual maturity. Generally, the first heat in ewe lambs of the mutton breeds occurs during the fall of their first year, when they are 8 to 10 months old.

Breeding Age

Most ewes are bred during the first breeding season after they are one year old, producing their first lambs when they are 2 years old.

Most sheepmen do not breed ewe lambs so that they drop their first lambs when they are one year old, even though this is possible, because it presents several problems including retarded growth, and reduction of birth weights of lambs. Also, more ewes require assistance at lambing, and more lambs are orphaned.

Heat Periods

The duration of estrus in ewes ranges from 3 to 70 hours, with an average of 28 hours. Unlike most animals, the ewe does not show outward signs to indicate heat, the acceptance of the ram being the only method. Ovulation seems to occur at about 24 hours from the onset of the heat period. If the ewe fails to settle, the heat cycle will recur after an interval of 14 to 19 days, with the average time being about 16 days. Ewes normally breed in late summer or early fall.

44

Gestation Period

The *gestation period* will vary between breeds of sheep and between individuals, but the normal range is between 144 to 152 days. The medium wool breeds have the shortest gestation period. Individuals in a breed may vary up to a range of 15 days.

Prolificacy in Ewes

Sheepmen have long considered that twinning in sheep is important. An old English adage states: "Ewes yearly by twinning rich masters do make, the lambs of such twinners for breeders go take." Twinning is an inherited characteristic, but not as much so as some other traits.

Prolificacy is largely determined by the number of eggs liberated by the ovary at the heat period. If only one egg is released and fertilized, a single lamb will be born, unless the egg divides and produces twins. This does not occur very often. Most twins and triplets are the result of multiple eggs being released and fertilized. The number of eggs shed depends on heredity, environment and age. Some breeds and strains produce a higher percentage of twins and triplets than others. The Finnsheep have high prolificacy, with triplets and quadruple births being common. Much work is now being done to crossbreed Finnsheep with other breeds that have more desirable wool and meat traits, and yet retain the prolificacy trait of the Finnsheep.

Certain environmental conditions, such as *"flushing"* the ewes, can be used to help increase the number of eggs released. Flushing is the practice of feeding ewes a larger and richer diet during a 2 to 3 week period immediately prior to breeding. This practice is believed to increase the lamb crop by 15 to 20 percent. Ewes will also breed earlier and more nearly at the same time. If the ewes are fat at breeding time, exercise is a good conditioner before breeding.

Practical observation indicates that age is a factor in twinning, with middle-age ewes producing more twins than either ewe lambs or very old ewes. The annual maintenance requirements of ewes are not very much different whether they produce one lamb or two. In any case, feed them adequately to achieve the best results.

45

High temperatures of 90° F. and over have a tendency to lower semen volume and quality. If you want early lambs, it will pay dividends to furnish shade and perhaps some type of cooling for the rams prior to and during the breeding period. Shearing the rams also helps.

Prior to the breeding season tag and trim the ewes about the dock in order to prevent the ewes from befouling themselves, and to remove obstacles for the ram. If you don't shear the ram at least clip the wool from his neck and belly. Trim the ram's hooves before the breeding season.

Marking

It pays to keep good records during the breeding season. The easiest way to keep a breeding record is to smear the ram's breast and the area between his forelegs every day or two with a thick paste made from grease and lamp black, venetian red or yellow ochre. Then, as the ram serves the ewe, a mark will be left on her rump. Don't use paint or tar for this purpose. If you change the color at about 16 day intervals, you can determine if ewes are returning to heat. If a good number of the ewes return to heat, replace the ram.

Keep stud rams separate from the ewes except during the breeding season. Some protection from inclement weather will be needed for the rams, with space for plenty of exercise. Excess fat may be harmful from a breeding standpoint; so don't overfeed.

Caring for the Ewe

Caring for the pregnant ewe is not exacting or different. She needs feed, water, exercise and a simple shelter.

Feeding the ewes is a most important factor in how well the lambs do. In general, this means feeding a suitable and well-balanced ration together with the necessary minerals and vitamins. Ewes should gain 15 to 25 pounds in weight during the entire period of pregnancy. They should enter the nursing period with some reserve of flesh, because the lactation period requirements are much more rigorous than those of the gestation period.

After the ewes have been bred, put them to pasture. Green rye, oats, or wheat furnish a very succulent feed, and the ewe will get valuable exercise. If possible, use stubble fields and stalk fields. If you don't have winter pastures, feed the ewes a good quality legume hay, such as alfalfa or clover. A 150 pound ewe will eat about 4 pounds of hay daily. If you feed grass hay, supplement it with about ¼ pound of cotton seed meal or soybean meal per day. About a month or 6 weeks before lambing, give the ewe ¾ to one pound of grain daily. If grain is not available, use a pelleted or cubed protein supplement. Not only will good feeding result in a strong, more vigorous lamb, but the ewe will milk better.

During periods of inclement weather and when ewes are fed in pens, they quite often do not exercise enough. As a result, they become sluggish and develop poor blood circulation. Force them to exercise by scattering feed some distance away or by driving the ewes at a moderate walk. Try to provide a shed-type shelter that will keep the ewes from becoming soaked with rain or wet snow, and a well-drained ground area that will stay dry. Because small acreage farms are normally located in built-up areas where dogs roam about, fence the pens to keep stray dogs away from the ewes.

At lambing time, the ewe needs to be watched carefully. As lambing time approaches, "tag" unsheared ewes by clipping the wool from around the udder, flank and dock. Reduce the grain ration or eliminate it completely, but continue the roughage. If you have not kept breeding records, you will have to rely on other signs of approaching *parturition* — the ewe will become uneasy and nervous, the area in front of the hips will begin to sink and the udder will become full and extended. When you notice these signs, move the ewe into a lambing pen. These pens are normally about 4 or 5 feet square, and are made up of portable panels that can be arranged along one side of the shelter wall.

Lambing pens are very important. They prevent other sheep from trampling on the new-born lamb, eliminate the possibility of the lamb wandering away and becoming chilled, and keep the lamb and ewe together, which cuts down on the number of disowned lambs. It is much easier for the ewe to raise the lamb than it is for you to bottle feed and raise orphan lambs.

There are times when ewes will need some help during birthing. This is especially true with young ewes having their first lambs. A good rule is to be near during parturition, but not to disturb the ewe unless she needs help. The normal presentation of the lamb consists of having the forelegs extended, with the head lying between them; sometimes, however, they are delivered breech, hind legs first. After the lamb is born, treat the navel with tincture of iodine.

Should the ewe labor for some time with little or no progress, it is usually a good idea to take the lamb. If the lamb is not in the proper position, insert your hand and arm in the vulva and turn the lamb so that the forefeet and head are in the proper position to be delivered first. You can help delivery by pulling the lamb outward **47** and downward as the ewe strains. Do not pull except when the ewe strains unless absolutely necessary. Keep warm water and soap, disinfectant, and petroleum jelly at the lambing pens, and use them before and after assistance is given to a ewe.

As soon as the lamb is born, give the ewe a chance to smell her lamb so she can identify it. Dry the lamb and keep it warm to prevent chilling. Allow it to nurse as soon as possible. Very often, even a very weak lamb will nurse the ewe if it is held to the teat. If necessary, milk the *colostrum* of the ewe, put the milk in a sterilized bottle, and feed the lamb a few teaspoons each hour by means of the bottle and nipple until it gains strength enough to get up and nurse on its own.

Sometimes a ewe will give birth to a lamb but will not start her milk flow. If this happens, get milk from another ewe that has just given birth because the lamb must have colostrum, which is the first milk the ewe gives and contains special antibodies the lamb must have to live and do well. Perhaps in a few hours the ewe will start her normal milk flow.

Caring for the Orphan Lamb

Because orphan lambs require a lot of time and effort to raise, every effort should be made to avoid having the ewe reject the newborn lamb. Strong, healthy ewes that have been properly fed and cared for during pregnancy are a lot less likely to have trouble lambing and to disown their lambs. Disowning lambs, for the most part, is due to improper feeding, a poor milk supply or an inflamed udder. Sometimes the maternal instinct is not developed. This is often true with ewes having their first lambs.

If a lamb is orphaned, first try to "graft" the lamb to another ewe. Ewes recognize their lambs the first few days by scent or sense of smell. Deception in the scent or sense of smell is then necessary if she is to accept another lamb. The most common practices are to milk some of the ewe's milk and put it on the rump of the lamb and smear some on the nose of the ewe, or take some of the mucus from the mouth and nose of the lamb, and smear it over the nose of the ewe. The ewe can be blindfolded so she cannot see the lamb. If you attempt to replace a dead lamb with one that has been orphaned, rub the lamb with the body of the dead lamb. If all these methods fail, you will have to raise the lamb on cow's or goat's milk.

48 During the first two days, feed the lamb ewe's milk that has *colostrum*, if at all possible. Feed the orphan 1 ounce of milk every 2 hours in a sterilized bottle heated to 100° F. Increase the quantity gradually, and space the intervals farther apart. Cow's milk is lower in butterfat and solids than ewe's milk or goat's milk, and should not be diluted.

Following parturition, the ewe will be in a feverish condition and should be handled carefully. Feed her water immediately and at regular intervals thereafter, but don't allow her to gorge herself. The water should not be cold. Feed her hay together with a little bran and oat mixture for the next few days.

Sheep Products

Sheep yield two products, lamb, or mutton, and wool. At the present time, the income from sheep is roughly 60% from lambs and 40% from wool. Despite the larger income from lambs it should be recognized that fleece does represent a certain income whether a lamb is produced or not.

Meat

The most common method of lamb production is to have the lambs arrive in the spring, raise them on grass and their mothers' milk, and then sell them in late summer either to the packer or as feeder lambs to go into a feed lot for additional feeding. Lambs that are dropped early are sometimes marketed at about 20 to 30 pounds as Easter lambs. The Easter trade is rather restricted, and will depend on location as much as anything. Young lambs marketed to packers before July 1st are known in the trade as spring lambs. After July 1st, this market classification no longer exists.

Try to have good succulent pasture available for the growing-fattening stage of lamb — the period extending from birth to weaning at 4 to 6 months of age. Most sheepmen consider a combination of green forage and the ewe's milk ample to market a fat lamb. In fact, lambs are unique among farm animals because they can be sold at top prices right off the grass and milk.

If pastures are dry and short, *creep-feeding* the lambs with grain can insure that they will be in condition to bring top prices at marketing; otherwise, the lambs must be sold to feeders. The business of feeding lambs is a special field, and not recommended for the mini farmer unless he has had a lot of experience in the sheep business.

49

Wool

Wool is the natural protective covering of sheep. It differs from other animal fibers by having a serrated surface. It has an excellent degree of elasticity and a wavy appearance. Chemically, wool is chiefly keratin, which is the same as hair, nails, hooves, horns and feathers.

Wool as it is shorn from the sheep is called *grease wool.* In a broad sense, grease refers to all the impurities found in unscoured wool. Although fleece shrinkage due to impurities varies widely, on the average farm flocks shorn, grease wool shrinks about 55% to 60%.

You should give proper care and attention to producing and handling the wool clip. If you've done a good job feeding and managing the flock, the sheep will have heavy fleeces with strong fibers. Periods of undernourishment caused by poor feed, diseases or parasites result in weak spots in the fiber. This is called "tender wool" in the trade, and the clip is discounted by the wool buyers. The use of insoluble paint on sheep for branding and marking also damages the wool, and buyers will reduce the price paid for such wool.

It is very difficult to keep all trash from the wool; however, make every effort to keep burrs, straw, chaff and manure from the wool clip because it is very difficult to remove mechanically in the textile mills, and buyers will discount heavily the prices paid for such wool. If you keep the hay in racks and mow weeds in the pasture, you will find it easier to keep the wool clean. Don't allow cocklebur and burdock to mature their burrs.

Shearing

Shearing sheep is largely a seasonal job. In the southwestern United States, many sheepmen start shearing in March, whereas in the north and northwest, shearing may be delayed until about the first of July. In general, the weather is the most important factor in determining when to shear. The fleece should not be removed until the danger of cold rains and snow is past. As the weather warms, the yolk becomes soft, and shears work better without "gumming up."

Another factor besides weather that determines shearing time is the availability of help. In some areas professional shearers follow the sheep ranges. However, most small acreage farmers will not be in such areas, and the shearing will have to be done with local help.

Lambing time can also determine when shearing is done. It is a good idea to shear before lambing, if you handle the ewes carefully. The lambs will normally do better when raised on ewes that are shorn before lambing. Delaying the shearing to obtain a heavier fleece does not really pay dividends because much of the increased weight is grease. The animal will rub off or otherwise lose part of the fleece if shearing is late.

Shear the sheep only when the wool is perfectly dry. The wool should also be stored in a dry place because damp wool will mildew and spoil. Remove all "tags" or lumps of manure before starting to shear. A good practice is to remove tags from time to time so that none are present at shearing time. The shearing area should be clean and dry. If you don't have a hard surface, use a canvas or old carpet for a shearing area.

Good shearing is a technique that must be developed. If possible, get a skilled shearer to give instructions in the proper techniques. If none is available, a motion picture of the subject is available from most state agricultural colleges. Some colleges have shearing classes that are presented as short courses during the summer months.

After you have collected the wool, tie the fleece with a special paper twine and pack it in a regulation wool bag. The bag is made from jute, and is 40 inches wide by 7½ feet long. Always pack the bag with the machine. Lock-stitch seams on the outside. The wool bag is opened by the workers by pulling the lock stitch in much the same manner as pulling open the top of a sack of feed. If the seam is on the inside, it is impossible to open the bag.

Grades of Wool

Many factors enter into the value of grease wool, but the most important are diameter and length. The fineness determines the grade; the length determines the class. There are two distinct methods of grading wool according to diameter, with several grades in each. The older method is called the "blood system"; the newer method is called the "wool-quality-number system."

The blood system derived its name from the amount of Merino breeding that the sheep had. The seven grades are (l) fine, (2) ½ blood, (3) 3/8 blood, (4) ¼ blood, (5) low ¼ blood, (6) common, and (7) braid. Fine refers to a full blood Merino. At the present time, these grades indicate the wool diameter, and have no connection whatsoever with the amount of Merino blood in the sheep.

The wool-quality-number system divides all wool into twelve grades, and each grade is designated by a number. The numbers range from 80, for the finest of wool, down to 36 for the coarsest. Theoretically, the system is based on the number of hanks of yarn (a hank is 560 yards) that can be spun from one pound of such wool.

Breeds of Sheep

No other class of livestock has evolved more breeds and types than the sheep class has. Of the more than 200 different breeds of sheep, many are of minor or local importance. Three-fourths of the world's commercial production is based on six breeds.

In the United States, the prevalent breeds within the six wool types are as follows:

1. **Fine Wool** American Merino, Delaine Merino, Rambouillet
2. **Medium Wool** Cheviot, Dorset, Hampshire, Oxford, Shropshire, Southdown Suffolk, Tunis
3. **Long Wool** Cotswold, Leicester, Lincoln, Rommy
4. **Crossbred Wool Type** Columbia, Corriedale, Panama, Romeldale, Targhee, Navajo
5. **Carpet Wool Type** Black Faced Highland
6. **Fur Type** Karakul

The four most popular breeds of registered sheep in the United States are Shropshire, Hampshire, Rambouillet, and Merino.

Fine Wool Breeds

The Merino Breed

The word *Merino* is derived from an early-day royal officer of Spain called the Merino, whose duty it was to assign the various migratory flocks of the country to their respective grazing grounds. At a very early date, Spain developed the Merino sheep, a type that produced wool of unusually fine fiber suitable for making fine cloth.

In Spain, the powerful nobility and clergy who were involved in the sheep industry wanted to produce the finest wool. The early flock masters drove their sheep from southern pastures to northern pastures in the spring and returned in the fall. In the migration process, any animal that failed to keep up with the band was left by the wayside. Presumably, this accounts for the flocking instinct and hardiness of the Merino.

Spain long held a monopoly on the Merino sheep. It was a criminal offense, punishable by death, for anyone to send a sheep of this breed out of Spain. The monopoly was broken when Napoleon invaded Spain and shipped Merino sheep to other countries.

1. **The American Merino.** This is known as the wrinkle type, because of its development of wrinkles. Sheep of this type are small. A mature ram weighs from 130 to 160 pounds, and ewes from 90 to 120 pounds.

2. **The Delaine Merino.** This is referred to as a smooth Merino. The word *Delaine* was derived from a French fabric that was made from the wool of these sheep. The Delaine Merino is a large animal, the rams weighing from 150 to 200 pounds, and the ewes from 110 to 150 pounds.

Merino Ram

53

Rambouillet

The Rambouillet is also a descendant of the Spanish Merinos. King Louis XVI of France purchased a small flock from the King of Spain, and from selective breeding developed a larger-sized, fine-wool type sheep. For many years grade Rambouillet dominated the commercial range sheep industry of the western United States, although recently the crossbred types have become more important. It has been estimated that 50% of the sheep in the United States carry some Rambouillet breeding.

Modern Rambouillet sheep are large, dual-purpose animals

that are rugged, fast-growing, and of acceptable mutton conformation. It is one of the breeds that the small acreage farmer should consider in his selection.

The mature ram in good condition and with full fleece weighs from 225 to 275 pounds, and ewes weigh from 140 to 200 pounds. Most rams have spiral horns, a white face, white legs and pink skin.

Rambouillet Ram

Medium Wool Breeds

Hampshire

The face, ears and legs of the Hampshire are a rich, deep brown, approaching black. To most people the color seems to be simply black. The sheep are polled, although some rams may have small scurs. The Hampshire is one of the largest of the medium wool breeds, with rams weighing 225 to 300 pounds, and ewes from 150 to 200 pounds. The head is large. They are heavy in the shoulders, but lack fullness in the rear quarters. As a breed, Hampshires are excellent *mutton-type sheep,* and shear a wool fleece of about 7 to 8 pounds.

The Hampshire breed is renowned for the rapid growth made by the lambs. Under good management, lambs usually will gain an average of one pound a day from birth until marketing age. The ewes are prolific and good milkers. Hampshire rams have been used to a great extent for crossbreeding; however, they are losing out to other breeds such as Suffolk, Columbia and Oxford.

Hampshire Ewe

Suffolk

The Suffolk is a very old breed; however, it did not get started in the United States until recent years. Commercial range sheepmen are using more and more Suffolk rams for crossing. The chief advantage is less trouble at lambing, as the Suffolk does not have the large head and shoulders of the Hampshire. Other advantages are that the lambs are free from wool blindness, and are better *rustlers.*

The most commanding characteristics of the Suffolk sheep are their very black faces, ears and legs. Their heads and ears are completely free of wool, with the black hair line extending to the base of the ears. There is no wool below the knees and hocks. The breed is alert and active. Both ewes and rams are polled.

The Suffolk sheep are large in size, the rams weighing 225 to 300 pounds, and ewes 160 to 225 pounds. Their most glaring deficiency is the light shearing of 6 to 7 pounds of wool. The ewes are very prolific and excellent milkers; they are good *hustlers* and grazers.

Shropshire

The Shropshire is very popular in the United States, but the wool blindness trait holds it back. The Shropshire is truly the "middle-of-the-road" breed noted for its profitable combination of mutton and wool qualities. The breed does not possess the qualities of the extreme mutton type, but it is thick, symmetrical, smooth and well fleshed. The fleece is quite heavy for the size of the animal. Clips of 10 pounds are not uncommon. The face, ears and legs are a deep, soft brown in color. Both sexes are polled. The

56

Shropshire Ram

rams weight from 175 to 250 pounds, and the ewes 135 to 175 pounds. The ewes are very prolific and are good milkers. A lamb crop of 150% is not unusual.

Southdown

The Southdown breed is the best mutton breed in the medium wool classification. The body of the Southdown is compact, very wide and deep. The legs are short, but full. The carcass quality is the best. From the standpoint of market maturity, Southdown lambs are unexcelled. For this reason, they are used extensively in cross-breeding for spring lambs. Their small size has kept them from being used for cross-breeding on the western ranges. The rams weigh 175 to 225 pounds, and ewes 125 to 160 pounds.

The preferred color of the face, ears and legs is a steel grey, but some variations do occur, ranging from light grey to light brown. The fleece is short and weighs from 5 to 7 pounds. The breed is polled. The ewes are not too prolific, and are about average milkers.

Southdown Ram

Dorset

The Dorset breed of sheep is distinct in that both sexes are horned. The ewes will breed out of season and are noted for their prolificacy and heavy milk production. These factors make the Dorset suited to the production of hothouse lambs and Easter lambs. Because most of the demand for early lambs is east of the Mississippi River, most of the Dorsets are raised there.

Among the Dorset characteristics are horns, white face, ears and legs that are free from wool, pink nostrils, lips and skin, and white hooves. The breed is medium size, with the rams weighing 175 to 250 pounds, and the ewes 125 to 175 pounds. The fleece is likely to be light.

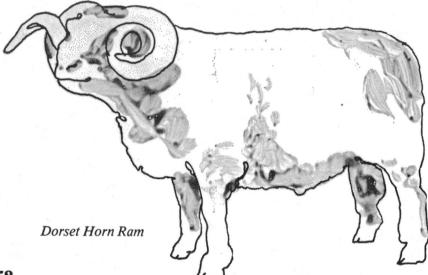

Dorset Horn Ram

Long Wool Breeds

The long wool breeds are used mainly for mutton production and are the largest of the sheep breeds. The Lincoln is the heaviest, with the rams weighing 250 to 350 pounds, and ewes 225 to 250 pounds. They are slow maturing sheep, and have long, coarse wool. The carcasses are coarse and overlaid with fat. In the United States, the meat is not readily accepted for this reason. Long wool sheep breeds have not been raised in any number in this country. Rams of some of the breeds have been used in crossbreeding programs to increase the size of other breeds.

Crossbred Wool Breeds

The crossbred breeds were developed from a long wool and fine wool foundation. This combination produced a breed that is often classed with the medium wool breeds. In general, the crossbred wool breeds, where bred to be adapted to the western range, are better producers than their parent stock or the regular medium wool breeds for that area.

Corriedale Breed

The Corriedale is the oldest of all the crossbred wool breeds. The Merino and Lincoln were the foundation stock from which the breed was established. By careful inbreeding and selection, a

59

Lincoln Ram

uniform type was established. The sheep were named Corriedale after the estate in New Zealand where the breed was established. The face, ears and legs are covered with white hair. Both sexes are polled. The rams weigh 185 to 250 pounds, and the ewes 125 to 185 pounds. On the average, the animal will shear 10 to 12 pounds of wool that grades 3/8 blood, and it is noted for exceptional length, brightness, softness and a very distinct crimp. The ewes are considered fair in prolificacy and milk production.

Columbia Breed

The Columbia breed is the first American breed developed. It is larger than other crossbreeds and is adapted for the better western ranges. A ram in good condition weighs from 225 to 275 pounds, and the ewes 125 to 190 pounds. Under range conditions, ewes will clip 11 to 13 pounds of grease wool, grading 3/8 and 1/4 blood. The lambs are of acceptable market type. The Columbia is open faced,with no tendency toward wool blindness. The face and legs are covered with white hair. Both sexes are polled. The ewes are above average in prolificacy and milking with good herding instincts.

Targhee Breed

The Targhee breed was developed in the United States by the Agricultural Research Service at Dubois, Idaho, using crosses of Rambouillet-Lincoln-Corriedales. This performance-selected strain is predominantly Rambouillet. It is a white-faced, polled breed of medium size. Rams weigh about 200 pounds, and ewes about 130 pounds. The wool clip will average about 11 pounds of half-blood quality.

Navajo Sheep

The Navajo Indian sheep are hairy, multicolored, unimproved sheep that are thought to be descendants of sheep brought to America by Cortez from Spain. They have some of the characteristics of the long wool sheep and some of the so-called carpet wool sheep.

HOGS

For many years pork has made a marked contribution to the economy of farmers and to the diet of Americans. The *hog* is unique among the larger farm animals because of its ability to convert grain into high protein meat at a ratio of one pound of meat produced for each four pounds of grain consumed. Only chickens and rabbits are more efficient at converting feed into meat. Compared to the hogs, cattle require twice as much grain to produce one pound of meat.

Approximately two-fifths of the meat eaten in the United States comes from hogs. While almost everyone is familiar with the mainstay items such as bacon, ham, sausage and pork chops, some may not realize that the hog also contributes lesser known, but most appetizing delicacies, such as pigs feet, hog jowls, hog stomach, kidneys, liver, tongue, head cheese and even brains. Almost every part of the hog is utilized after slaughter. It is often said that the only useless part of the hog is its squeal!

61

A very important factor favoring pork production on small farms is that the meat can be cured and stored better than other meats. At the present time, 80 per cent or more of the hog carcass is converted by various curing processes into nearly non-perishable forms. More pork is home cured than all other meats combined.

Hog production is well suited to the small farm because it requires a small investment to purchase stock, little additional labor, small space, and inexpensive equipment. Hogs also make excellent projects for youngsters involved in 4H and FFA organizations.

The small farm, if located in the right area, can have the capability of producing large numbers of hogs. Space in itself is not a major requirement, since hogs are raised in close confinement; however, you must control odors if the farm is located in a populated area, and from this standpoint, spacing is important. In some locations ordinances prohibit keeping hogs. Check all local ordinances before any decision is made to raise them.

Hogs are normally raised in large numbers where acreages of corn or other grains are large. More than one-half of the hogs produced in the United States are centered in the seven Corn Belt States. It should not be concluded from this, however, that other sections are not well adapted to pork production. As a matter of fact, an area that produces dairy by-products, small grains, and high quality forage can be adapted to the production of hogs. Although hogs require primarily concentrates for feed, they are excellent scavengers of waste such as skim milk, leftover bread, table scraps, etc. In fact, many small farmers keep one or two pigs to dispose of otherwise wasted products and to furnish them with their own pork. Hogs have been known throughout the country as the farm "mortgage lifters." No other animal has been of such importance to the American farmer.

With cattle, and to a lesser extent sheep, there is considerable "two-phase production" in which the young are produced on the ranges of the west, and then shipped to the Corn Belt as feeder animals to be fattened out on grain. This has not been the case with hogs. Until recently, the *farrowing,* raising and fattening process has been carried out on the same farm.

Recently a trend has developed to produce large numbers of *pigs* in *confinement* buildings. The nursery operations are carried on in total confinement. Pigs produced in these large specialized facilities are then sold to farmers for finishing. However, these operations still tend to be located in the areas of high grain production. If you are interested in such an operation, investigate the feed availability, and the market for feeder pigs in your area before becoming too deeply involved.

The following is a list of factors you can use to help determine if conditions are favorable for hog production.

Favorable Factors

1. Hogs excel over all other animals in the economy with which they convert concentrated feed into meat. It requires almost twice as much grain to obtain one pound of beef in the feed lot as it does to produce one pound of pork.
2. Hogs are prolific, commonly *farrowing* from 6 to 12 pigs, and producing two litters a year.
3. Hogs provide an excellent dressing percentage, yielding 65% to 80% of their live weight when dressed packer style. Moreover, because of the small proportion of bone, the percentage of edible meat in the carcass is larger.
4. Hogs are efficient converters of waste and by-products.
5. With proper equipment, labor can be kept to a minimum.
6. A small investment is all that is required for facilities and breeding stock.
7. Hog raising provides a quick return on investment. A *gilt* may be bred at 8 months and the pigs marketed 5 to 6 months after farrowing.
8. Markets are readily available throughout the country.

Unfavorable Factors

1. Hogs require a maximum of concentrates. Grain must be available without paying high transportation costs.
2. Hogs are susceptible to numerous diseases and parasites. Losses can be extremely high if disease strikes.
3. Odor control is now a must, and in some areas the cost of control is prohibitive.
4. Hogs require attention daily, almost constantly when *sows* are farrowing.
5. Hogs can destroy a pasture with rooting and grazing habits.

Establishing the Herd

Getting started with a hog herd is very similar to establishing a beef cattle or sheep herd. In general, however, one can establish a herd of hogs at a lower cost, and much more quickly. For maximum profit and satisfaction, consider the type, breeding and individual merit of each animal in the foundation herd and the size of the herd.

Good Conformation

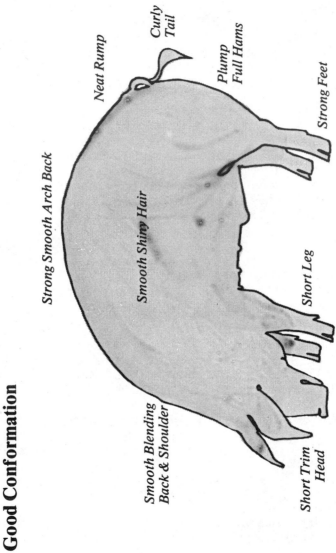

Strong Smooth Arch Back

Neat Rump

Curly Tail

Plump Full Hams

Strong Feet

Smooth Shiny Hair

Short Leg

Smooth Blending Back & Shoulder

Short Trim Head

Common Faults

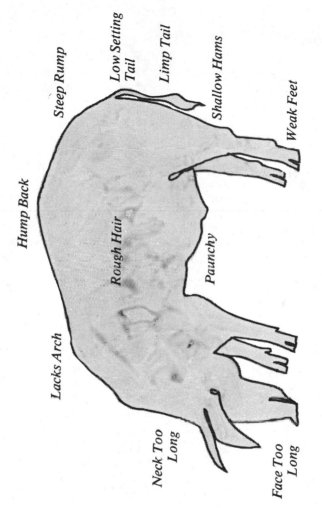

Steep Rump

Low Setting Tail

Limp Tail

Shallow Hams

Weak Feet

Hump Back

Rough Hair

Paunchy

Lacks Arch

Neck Too Long

Face Too Long

65

Generally speaking, do not try to produce purebreds until you have gained experience raising hogs. When you purchase your foundation stock, it is certainly worth considering purebred gilts instead of grade gilts, as in many cases the price difference is so small as to warrant purebreds even for commercial production. In any event, a purebred *boar* is always a good idea.

Hogs multiply more rapidly than any other class of farm animal. They also breed at an early age, produce twice each year, and bear litters. It does not take long to get into the hog business.

Type of Hogs

With reference to hogs, the word *type* is used in two ways: (l) to denote whether the breed is of the *meat-type* or *bacon-type;* and (2) to denote the difference in form and general *conformation* within a breed on the basis of large, medium, or small type. The shift to producing meat hogs instead of heavy lard types has brought the breeds more closely approaching the so-called bacon type. In addition, the use of bacon-type crossbreeding with meat-type hogs has found increasing favor in this country in recent years. Lard has become a "drag" on the market, often selling for less per pound than the price of live hogs. Today's hog producers prefer a meat type that is prolific and fast maturing.

Selecting the Breed

The beginner should start in a conservative way. This does not mean you should purchase poor quality animals, as they can prove to be expensive at any cost, but you should purchase one or two bred gilts that are well developed, uniform in type, and of good ancestry, and that have been mated to a "proved" boar. If you do this, you will usually have a wider selection purchase younger animals with longer useful lives.

66 Selecting the breed is primarily based on the personal preference of the producer. No breed of hogs can be said to excel in all points of production and for all conditions, although certain breed characteristics may be better adapted to a given set of conditions. For example, white hogs are subject to sun scald in the South and arid Southwest, and therefore are not as well adapted to these areas as the darker breeds. Usually there is as much or more difference among hogs of the same breed as there is among different breeds. If you don't have a definite preference, choose the breed that is most popular in the surrounding area. It will give greater latitude in the choice of individual animals for the herd, and create fewer problems in securing the services of a boar.

Generally, the selection of *foundation hogs* is made on the basis of one or more of the following considerations: (1) type or individuality, (2) pedigree, or (3) production testing.

In selecting individual animals, the nearer they approach the ideal, or standard of perfection, the better. The meat-type hog that is in demand today should be smooth, good sized, and have the ability to fatten during the growing period without producing excessive amounts of lard. The head and neck should be trim and neat; the back well arched and of ample width; the side long, deep and smooth; the hams well developed and deep. The legs should be medium length, straight, true and squarely set. The bones should be ample and show quality; the pasterns (joints above hooves) should be strong, with the animal standing upright on its hooves. The brood sows should show the feminine qualities of the breed; the udder should be well developed, carrying 10 to 12 teats.

Since no animal will be perfect, recognize and weigh the good and bad points. Never use the pedigree as the sole factor in selecting for the herd, although it should lend confidence in projecting how well the animal will do in the herd. Breeding animals of known merit are not usually available at prices that beginners are able to pay. Sometimes breeders to dispose of brood sows of proved performance to make way for younger stock, and sell proved boars because they can no longer be used in the breeding program. Animals of this kind can be one of the soundest investments a beginner can make.

Breeding

Because hogs are raised in confinement, breeders have been able to collect a considerable amount of knowledge about their breeding habits, maybe more than any other farm animal.

Puberty

The age of puberty in swine varies from 4 to 6 months. This wide range is due to differences in breeds, sex and environment, and especially nutrition. In general, boars (males) do not reach puberty as early as gilts (females less than 1-year old). The gilt that is well developed may be bred to farrow at 12 or 14 months of age. This depends on size and development rather than age. It is advantageous to breed the gilts reasonably early, as this establishes regular and reliable breeding habits.

Gestation Period

The heat period (the time the sow will accept the boar) lasts from 2 to 3 days on the average. Ovulation (the time the eggs are released) normally occurs on the second day of heat. If bred at this time, the sows are more likely to conceive than if bred at any other time of the heat period. If the sow is not bred, the heat period will recur at 21-day intervals, plus or minus a day or so. The external signs of heat in the sow are restless activity, swelling of the vulva, loud grunting and riding of other sows.

The average *gestation period* of sows is 114 days. The sow will often come into heat during the first few days after farrowing, but don't breed her back that soon. It is better to wean the pigs and give the sow a few days rest before rebreeding her. The normal breeding seasons for sows seem to be in the early summer and late autumn; however, they will breed at any time of the year. It is an advantage to have the sows farrow in the spring and fall. At these times of the year, the weather is milder, the pigs have less trouble with chills and they are less likely to be crushed by the sow. Extreme heat is hard on the sow when farrowing in hot weather, and the pigs do not grow off as well.

Prolificacy

A high degree of fertility and prolificacy is much desired. The cost of caring for a litter of 10 pigs is very little more than for 5 or 6. The maintenance cost of keeping the sow and boar remains fairly constant.

Low fertility in hogs is most commonly attributed to hereditary or environmental factors. Some breeds and strains of hogs are simply more prolific than others. The bacon breeds tend to be more prolific. Summer heat seems to lower prolificacy in hogs. Litter size is affected little, if any, by the boar. This would not be true if the boar were on the borderline of sterility, with insufficient viable sperm present to fertilize the eggs.

The practice of *flushing* the sows, helps to increase egg shed, encourages the sows to come into heat, and helps ensure conception. If the sows are already overly fat, the best preparation is plenty of exercise and access to lush pasture, while decreasing the amount of grain being fed.

Caring for the Pregnant Sow

Feeding

When you feed the sow, provide a ration which will insure her complete nourishment and that of her developing fetal litter, and choose the feeds and a method of feeding which will prove economical and adaptable to local farm conditions. If the gilt is not fully mature, provide nutrients for maternal growth as well as for fetal growth. Quality and quantity of proteins, minerals and vitamins become particularly important in the ration of young pregnant gilts. Their requirements are much greater and more exacting than those of the mature sow. The demands are greater in the last month of pregnancy because 2/3 of the growth of the fetus is made during that month. During gestation, it is necessary to build up body reserves for subsequent use during lactation. A sow that has a large litter and is a heavy milker will have a demand greater than can be supplied by the ration fed during lactation. A mature sow should gain about 75 to 85 pounds during the pregnancy period; gilts somewhat more.

The best place to keep the pregnant sow during the gestation period is on green pasture — one that has legumes such as alfalfa or clovers is the best. In addition to supplying low cost protein, the pasture will also enable the sow to get much needed exercise. In winter, the protein, mineral and vitamin requirements can be met by including 15% to 30% high quality ground alfalfa in the ration. The pregnant sow also should have free access to a three compartment mineral box, with salt in one compartment, steamed bone meal in another, and oyster shell flour or limestone in the third.

Hogs do very well on many different *concentrates*. This means you can choose ingredients for the rations that are readily available at the lowest price. If all other factors are equal, a variety of ingredients is preferable.

The listed ration for gestating sows provides over and above the minimum protein requirement for a margin of safety. Gestating sows are generally hand-fed to limit feed intake. This avoids excess fatness and unnecessary feed expense. However, they may be self-fed if more bulk is added to the ration; oats or 25% or more of ground alfalfa can be added.

| Ingredient | Sows in Dry Lot | | On Pasture |
	Ration #1 (lb)	Ration #2 (lb)	Ration #3 (lb)
Ground corn, wheat barley, oats, and/or sorghum	75	60	90
Alfalfa meal	15	30	
Animal Protein (tankage, meat meal, fish meal, and/or milk	6	5	5
Plant Protein (soybean, cotton seed, linseed, and/or peanut meals)	4	5	5

The mature pregnant sow should be limited to 1½ pounds of concentrate per 100 pounds of body weight per day. Replacement gilts should be limited to 2 pounds per day per 100 pounds of live weight. Ration #1 is for hand-feeding, Ration #2 is for self-feeding, and Ration #3 is supplemented feeding of hogs on pasture.

These rations are suitable for lactating sows. They will, however, consume from 2½ to 4½ pounds of concentrates daily for each 100 pounds of live weight, the mature sows on the lower side and the gilts in the upper range. In general, oats should not make up more than 1/3 of the rations.

Exercise

In addition to proper nutrition, be sure the pregnant sow has regular and careful exercise. If necessary, drive the sow at a moderate walk. Sows that have been exercised do not have as many problems at farrowing time.

Farrowing

As the farrowing time approaches, the sow becomes extremely nervous and uneasy. The vulva enlarges, and a mucous discharge is possible. At this time isolate the sow from the rest of the herd. Before the sow is moved into the farrowing quarter, scrub her down with soap and warm water, especially the under surface, udders and sides. Use a weak solution of disinfectant to rinse the sow off and to clean the farrowing crate, house and equipment.

Hogs are sensitive to extremes in weather conditions. The satisfactory farrowing house should be clean, dry and well ventilated. The house should give protection from heat, cold and wind; newborn pigs must be protected. It is estimated that 30% of the pigs farrowed do not reach weaning age. If you don't use farrowing crates, construct a guard rail around the farrowing pen to protect the pigs from being crushed by the sow. This simple rail is very important because half of the pigs that are lost are crushed by sows.

70 The rail should be 8 to 10 inches from the floor, and 8 to 12 inches from the walls. It can be constructed of 2 x 4's, 2 x 6's or iron pipe. Farrowing crates have proved much more satisfactory than pens. Some type of bedding material should be furnished; clean, chopped straw or hay is satisfactory.

Watch the sow at farrowing. You might need to free the newborn pigs from the enveloping membrane and get them started nursing. In cold weather, dry the pigs to avoid chilling.

If the sow has trouble at labor, give help. In such case, insert the hand and arm into the vulva and remove the pigs. Be sure that the fingernails are trimmed close, and the hand and arm are thoroughly washed with soap and water. Use a mild disinfectant, and lubricate the hand and arm with petroleum jelly. After delivery, be sure to wash and disinfect the hand and arm again.

As soon as the afterbirth is expelled, remove it from the pen, along with any dead pigs. It is an inherited trait that sows eat the afterbirth. This trait was probably developed to discourage predators; however, it also seems to encourage eating the pigs.

Caring for Baby Pigs

During cold weather, artificial heat must be provided. Most farrowing houses in the northern part of the United States are equipped with heat. Individual houses are usually equipped with an electric brooder-type heater. In the warmer areas, a simple heat lamp may be all that is required. Pigs that are farrowed during cold weather are easily chilled. If the pig becomes chilled, immerse the body, except for the head, in water that is about 100°F. for a few minutes, and then remove and dry by rubbing vigorously with cloths. Get the pigs nursing as soon as possible.

During the warm seasons, the best place for the sow and her litter is outside in the sunshine on pasture. The pasture area should be plowed if hogs were previously confined on it. A-frame individual houses usually are used to furnish shelter.

The pigs have eight small needle teeth when they are born; two on each side, top and bottom. Because these needle teeth are of no benefit, remove them to prevent scratches to the sow's udder and to each other. The needle teeth are easy to remove with a pair of pliers or side cutters. This should be done soon after birth.

To simplify identification and record keeping when more than one litter is kept together, notch the pigs' ears. You can do this with a special ear-marking tool, or with a leather punch. There is no set system; each breeder makes up his own system.

The male pigs that are not going to be kept for breeding purposes should be castrated. Do this in time for the wound to heal before the pigs are weaned. Do not feed the pigs for 8 or 10 hours prior to castration. Before performing the operation, wash the knife, hands, and the scrotum of the pig with disinfectant. Make sure the knife is sharp. Holding the scrotum in one hand with enough pressure to slightly stretch the skin, make an incision downward and extend it far enough so that the wound will drain well. Pop the testicles out and either pull or scrape the cord with the knife. Do not cut the cord sharply with the knife. Try not to excite the pigs any more than is necessary. Where possible, have the pigs penned in a small pen to minimize the need to run or chase them around. Also, keep the sow away. Some sows really get mean when their pigs are handled. Always be cautious when working around a sow, especially when she has a litter of pigs.

Caring for the Boar

Proper care and management of the herd *boars* is most essential for successful hog production. Sometimes the boar is neglected, put in a small, dirty pen with little chance to exercise, and improperly fed.

Outdoor exercise throughout the year is one of the essentials for proper conditioning of the boar. Provide enough feed to keep the boar in a thrifty, vigorous condition at all times. Being too fat is as much, or more, a problem as being too thin.

The number of services the boar is allowed to perform will vary with his age and condition and with the system used in mating. The boar should be at least 8 months old and well developed before being put into service. At that age, he should be capable of performing limited service of one a day during the breeding season, or approximately 24 services. A mature boar of 1 to 4 years should be capable of servicing twice a day during the breeding season. A boar that is well cared for and properly managed should be able to provide service for 6 or 8 years.

Numbers of Litters

You need to decide whether to have sows farrow one or two litters each year.

Advantages
1. Maximum use is made of the capital invested in facilities and equipment.
2. The two litter system makes it possible to retain outstanding sows in the breeding herd.
3. There is a more even distribution of labor.
4. Pigs are marketed twice a year which distributes income better
5. The maintenance cost of keeping the boar and sows is less per pig raised.

Disadvantages
1. In the northern latitudes, pigs arrive early in the spring while the weather is still cold. This contributes to higher pig losses.
2. Fall litters require more feed because pastures are not available.

Housing

Hog production is an area where the small acreage farmer can choose just how large an operation he wants to develop — from raising one hog for family meat to having a total system that produces hundreds of hogs from start to finish.

Small Operation

The first thing to consider in building any type of facility is that extreme temperatures, either hot or cold, increase the amount of feed required. Hogs are more efficient producers at temperatures in the 60° to 80° F. range. At either 35° or 90° F., the feed required to produce one hundred pounds of gain can double.

If you raise one or two pigs at a time, all you will need is a small pen with a shelter from the weather, a feeder and a water trough. Waste isn't a problem at this level, but the pen should be located far enough away from dwellings so that odors do not present a problem. Pigs raised on pasture seldom cause odor problems.

Confinement Housing

As the hog producer reaches the commercial level of production, the facilities requirements change. In recent years a trend has developed for raising hogs in total confinement. This system requires controlled-environment housing to keep in check extreme fluctuations of temperature, humidity, air velocities, air purity and solar radiation. In addition, a system of waste management must be designed to keep down odors and pollution.

The confinement system is expensive to build, but it does offer the small acreage farmer with a small amount of land a way to get into the hog business on a large scale. In addition, the confinement system has other advantages:

1. Less labor required per pig raised.
2. Better adapted to mechanical equipment.
3. Less feed per pound of gain.
4. More pigs saved at farrowing.
5. Better health for the herd.

In a total confinement environment, the operations are usually divided into four areas or buildings.

Total Confinement System

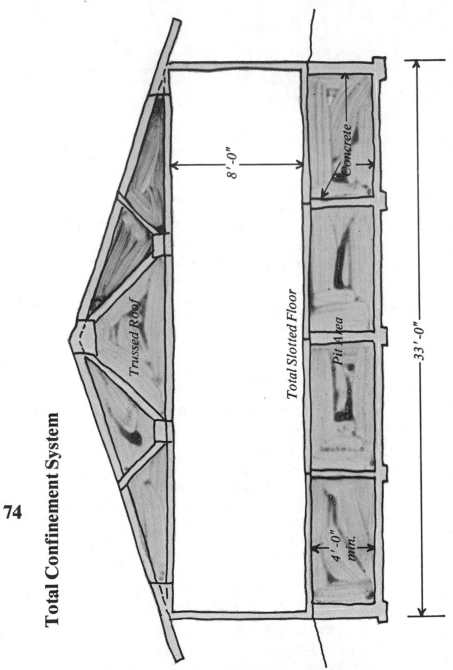

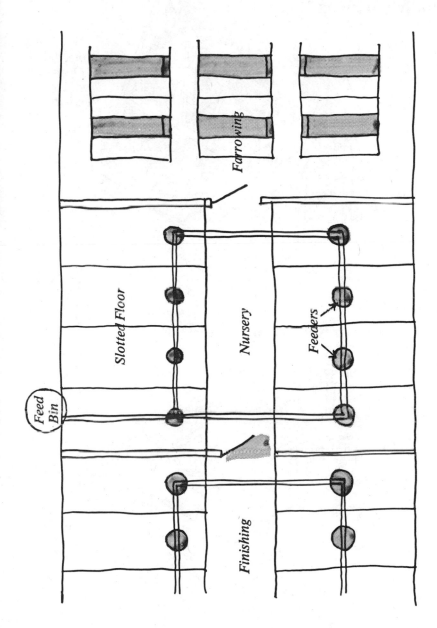

75

"A" Frame
Individual Hog House

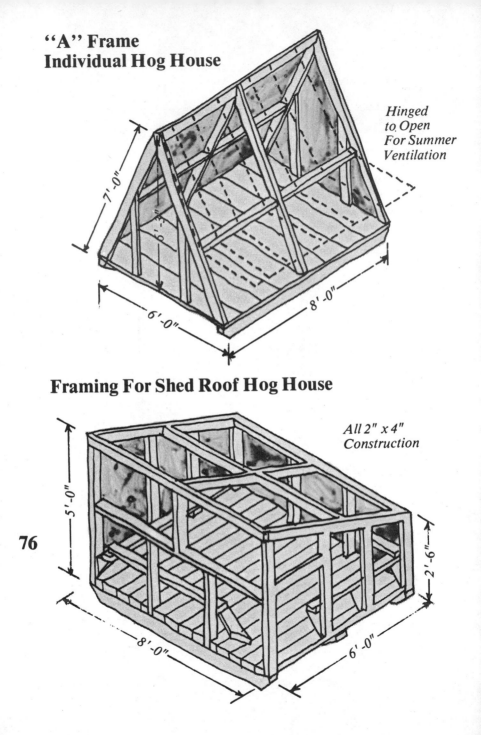

Hinged to Open For Summer Ventilation

7'-0"

6'-0"

8'-0"

Framing For Shed Roof Hog House

All 2" x 4" Construction

5'-0"

2'-6"

8'-0"

6'-0"

76

Farrowing House

This is a warm building where the pigs are born and cared for until weaning time, normally 2 to 5 weeks. A closed building for farrowing is recommended as small pigs must be kept warm, dry and free from drafts. Supplemental heat must be supplied in the pig brooder. Farrowing crates are usually used in the building to confine the sow. The crates are about 2 ft. wide and 7 or 8 ft. long. Farrowing crates can be used in most buildings, except open types, and are especially adapted to controlled environment housing.

Nursery

This is a separate building or a separate section of a building which provides warm, dry draft-free housing for pigs until weaning age. They should be ready to move to the finish building at 8 to 10 weeks of age, or at 40 to 60 pounds. Open-type buildings are not recommended. Controlled environment housing with slotted floors is recommended, with 3 to 4 sq. ft. per pig.

Finishing House

This is a building or area where pigs are grown from nursery age to market weight, usually 5 to 6 months of age. In planning the finishing house, provide for temperature control with the ventilation system. Controlled environment is recommended for the North Central states. Slotted floors, or partially slotted floors, should be included to greatly reduce the daily chore of cleaning. Divide the building into pens of 6 ft. by 16 ft., or 4 ft. by 12 ft. Keep animals of the same size together in the pens. Bulk feed storage with mechanical conveyor to deliver feed to pen feeders will greatly reduce the amount of labor. Locate the water cup over a slotted area.

Breeding Stock House

This is the area where the sows, gilts and boars are kept. In some operations, the sows and gilts are kept outside on pasture so they can benefit from grazing and proper exercise. In other operations, all animals are maintained in small pens inside the building.

It is still considered good practice to pasture sows and gilts during gestation, except in extreme weather conditions. Provide a shelter area of 30 sq. ft. per sow in cold weather, and a water spray to wet and cool the sows in hot weather.

The breeding herd should always be housed separately from the rest of the herd. Farrowing and the nursery can be housed together in the same building. Some new units are being built that include the facilities for complete production from farrowing to finishing all in one total confinement building.

Farrowing Crate

*All Metal
Construction*

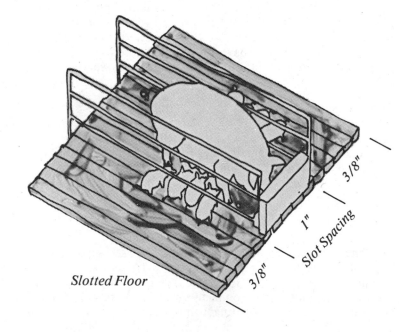

Slotted Floor

3/8"

1"

Slot Spacing

3/8"

Fattening Hogs for Market

Pigs are normally weaned from 6 to 10 weeks with 8 weeks being the most preferred time. The pigs then enter the "growing-fattening" stage until they reach about 225 pounds, the average market weight. Because hogs are fattened at an early age, the process consists of both growing and fattening. In general there are two methods of finishing hogs for market:

1. Fully feeding all the time until the animals attain a market weight, usually in 5 to 6 months. This is usually accomplished in dry lot or total confinement.

2. Limited feeding early in the period with full feeding the last 60 to 75 days of the period before marketing. Pastures are usually used in combination with dry lots with this method.

The method you use should be determined by (a) available pasture, (b) time of the year, (c) market conditions, (d) available feed on the farm, and (e) price of feed.

When on full feed, pigs that are being fattened will consume approximately 5 pounds of feed daily per 100 pounds of live weight up to 100 pounds in weight. On the average, about 400 pounds of feed is required to produce 100 pounds of gain during the growing-fattening period. About 360 pounds of this feed is grain and 40 pounds is protein supplement, about one-half plant and one-half animal protein.

Protein Requirements

Pigs need protein the most early in life. For this reason, incorporate decreasing percentages of protein supplement in the feeds as the following table indicates:

Range in Weight of Pigs	% Protein Content in the Ration
Weaning to 75 pounds	20
75 to 125 pounds	16
125 to 225 pounds	14

Mineral Requirements

Of all common farm animals, the pig is most likely to suffer from mineral deficiencies. This is because they are fed principally with cereal grains that are low in mineral content. The skeleton of the pig supports greater weight in proportion to its size than other farm animals, and they grow more rapidly.

If you use pre-mixed feed rations, most will be supplied with the proper minerals and vitamins. Always check the ration mixture however, to insure that the normal requirements are being met. You might want to give hogs free access to required minerals by providing them in a suitable self-feeder. Salt should be provided in a separate compartment.

Rations

The following tables can be used as a guide for rations of growing-fattening pigs:

For Dry Lot Pigs

Ingredients-lb. in 100 wt.	Under 75 Ration #1	75-100 #2	Pig Weight 100-150 #3 (lb.)	150-200 #4	200-250 #5
Ground corn, oats, barley and/or sorghum	58	77	80	83	86
Alfalfa Meal	6	8	9	9	6
Animal Protein	18	7	5	4	4
Plant Protein	18	8	6	4	4

For Pigs on Pasture

Ingredients-lb. in 100 wt.	Under 75 Ration #1	75-100 #2	Pig Weight 100-150 #3 (lb.)	150-200 #4	200-250 #5
Ground corn, oats, barley and/or sorghum	72	82	89	95	95
Animal Protein	14	9	5½	2½	2½
Plant Protein	14	9	5½	2½	2½

You can substitute feeds of similar nutritive value as the price relationships warrant. Some of these feeds are cereal grains (wheat, corn, oats, barley and grain sorghum), animal proteins (tankage, meat meal, fish meal and dried milk), and plant proteins (soybean, cottonseed, linseed and peanut meal). If you use wheat, barley, oats and/or grain sorghum instead of corn, you can reduce the plant protein supplement slightly. These grains are higher in protein than corn.

Parasites and Diseases

The prevention of diseases is an important part of a good hog management program. Good sanitation is probably the key factor to controlling the insects and diseases that affect hogs. Most hogs are raised in close confinement in somewhat crowded quarters. This tends to lower their resistance to disease, and causes the disease to spread once it has started.

Sanitation Practices

Modern management practices have proved that hogs thrive and grow better when they are raised in a clean environment. The days of allowing hogs to feed on filthy feeding floors, to drink from dirty water troughs, or to bed down in wet, filthy or dusty bedding places has ended. The idea that a hog should have a mud hole in which to wallow is completely without foundation. Actually, hogs keep themselves cleaner than most other farm animals if given the opportunity to do so. If you need cooling facilities, install a water spray system over a concrete slab with a shed type roof.

Do not allow manure and litter to accumulate in the hog houses or pens. Plow hog pasture areas periodically by turning under all the accumulated debris. Then sow the pasture with rye, wheat, rape or similar crop.

The central hog houses should have concrete floors with drains so that the floors can be washed down with water to keep them clean. Always use a good disinfectant before each new herd is brought into the houses. Several disinfectants on the market do a satisfactory job, but the old standby of one pound of lye to 10 to 20 gallons of water is very effective. Add a sufficient amount of hydrated lime to the disinfectant to make a thin whitewash, enabling you to detect any part of the surface that may have been missed. Use a pump with sufficient pressure to force the disinfectant into all cracks and crevices.

Good, clean water should be available to the hogs at all times. An automatic drinking fountain that furnishes water only when the hog operates it with his snout (which he will learn to do in short order) is preferable. Ponds and wallows are little better than cesspools and should never be relied on to provide drinking water. As a matter of fact, they should be filled in with dirt to prevent the hogs from using them for drinking water.

Use self-feeders if at all possible. They are much more sanitary and waste less feed. If you plan to hand-feed the hogs, be sure the germ than the one which causes Bang's disease in cattle or Malta fever in goats. This disease causes pregnant sows and gilts to abort their feti before the normal farrowing time. The entire herd should be blood tested when an infection of this type occurs. Only animals that show negative results should be retained in the breeding herd.

Breeds of Hogs

Hogs were first domesticated in China in the Neolithic times. The first domestic pig was the East Indian pig. Later, the European wild boar was domesticated. These two wild stocks contributed the ancestry for the present American breeds of hogs.

The most thoroughly American domestic animal is the hog. In no other class of animals have so many truly American breeds been created. The American hog raiser has taken the mongrel sow descended from colonial ancestry as a base, and crossed her with imported Chinese, Neapolitan, Berkshire, Tamworth, Russian, Suffolk Black, Byfield and Irish Grazier boars. Out of the various crosses, which varied from area to area, were created the several genuinely American breeds of hogs adapted to the climate and feeds available in the United States. One of the most noted changes has been in the digestive tract. The American breeds now have a digestive tract that is 13.5 to 1 compared with his body length, whereas the proportion to body length of the wild boar is only 9 to 1. This enables the American breeds to consume more feed for conversion into meat.

The most common breeds of hogs in the United States are the Berkshire, Chester White, Duroc, Hampshire, Hereford, OIC, Poland China, Spotted Poland China, Tamsworth (bacon type), and Yorkshire (bacon type). With the exception of Berkshire, Tamsworth and Yorkshire, these breeds are strictly American creations. However, American breeds were not developed without recourse to foreign stock, because none of the parent stock was native to America.

84

In the hands of a skilled geneticist, the conformation of the hog herd can be completely changed in 4 or 5 years. Hogs are the most plastic of any species of farm animals.

The Berkshire Breed

The Berkshire is a native of England. The distinct peculiarity of the Berkshire is the short, upturned nose. The face is dished, and the ears are erect but inclined slightly forward. The color is black with six white points, four white feet, some white on the face, and a white switch on the tail. The meat is exceptionally fine in quality, well streaked with lean, and has no heavy covering of fat.

The Berkshire is smaller than most other breeds. However, because of its "chunky" appearance it may weigh more than expected. It is long bodied and has good depth. The sows tend to be on the lower end of the scale with litter sizes. However, they exhibit good mothering instincts and are good milkers.

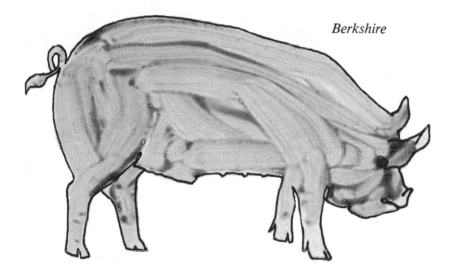

Berkshire

85

The Chester White Breed

The Chester White is a very popular breed on farms in the northern part of the United States. The Chester White had its origin in eastern Pennsylvania.

As the name indicates, the breed is white in color. Its light color has caused it to be subject to sun scalds in the south and southwestern United States. The Chester White breed is a medium-sized animal with a long, smooth body, medium nose, and forward droopy ears. It stands fairly well up on its legs. The sows are very prolific and are exceptional mothers. The pigs are good feeders and grazers.

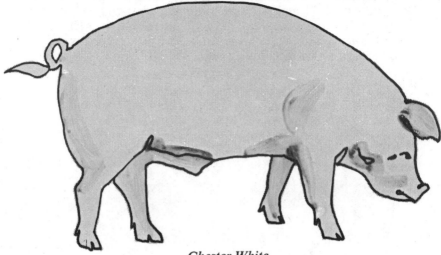

Chester White

The Duroc Breed

The Duroc hogs originated in the northeastern United States. The hogs, of uncertain origin, were found in that area and were named after a famous red stallion, Duroc, a noted horse of the day. The color of these hogs is even similar to the stallion's.

The Duroc is red in color; with shades varying from light to dark, although the medium cherry red is preferred. The great popularity of the breed is attributed to the combination of size, feeding capacity, prolificacy and hardiness. In show condition, a Duroc boar may weigh as much as 1000 to 1100 pounds, and a mature sow from 600 to 850 pounds.

The Hampshire Breed

The Hampshire is one of the youngest breeds of hogs. It originated in Boone County, Kentucky. The most striking characteristic of the Hampshire is the white belt around the shoulders and body, including the front legs. The black color with this white belt marking is a distinctive trademark.

The breed stresses great quality and smoothness. The jowl is trim and light, the ears are erect and the back carries a good smooth arch. The body is long, and the animal stands high on long legs. The Hampshires are not as heavy as the other breeds. In show condition, a mature boar weighs from 700 to 900 pounds, and a mature sow from 550 to 750 pounds.

The Hampshires are active, and the sows have a reputation for farrowing large litters and raising a high percentage of the pigs farrowed.

Hampshire

87

The Hereford Breed

The Hereford hog is a recently developed breed. The idea behind the breeding was a cherry-red body with white markings that resembled the Hereford cattle. The ideal colored Hereford hog has a white head and ears, four white feet, white switch, and white markings on the under body. The remainder of the body is cherry red. The Hereford is smaller in size than the other breeds, and it tends to be a little "chunky" or "lardy."

The OIC Breed

The OIC breed was started from selected animals from the Chester Whites. The OIC name was derived from Ohio Improved Chester. Through years of selective breeding, it is now established as a separate breed. Supposedly they are larger and more prolific than Chester Whites; however, they tend to be chubby.

The Poland China Breed

The Poland China breed originated in Ohio's fertile Miami Valley. The breed's characteristics are a black color with six white points — the feet, face, and tail tip. They are compact and short legged, have droopy ears and are fine meat animals. There is a strain of large bone and a strain of small bone; however, both strains of the breed are fairly large animals. Mature boars weigh from 850 to 1000 .pounds, and mature sows from 650 to 900 pounds.

Poland China

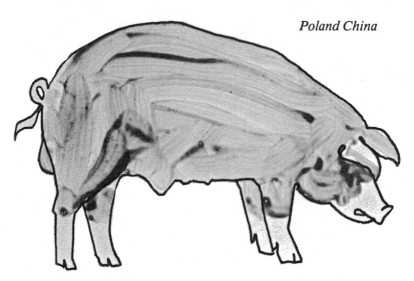

88

The Spotted Poland China Breed

The Spotted Poland China breed is a selection going way back in the breed's history when both the standard Poland China and the

Spotted Poland China were considered the same breed. The Gloucester Spotted hog from England was introduced into the breed in later years. At the present time there is very little difference in conformation between the two breeds. The Spotted Poland Chinas are perhaps slightly smaller. The desired color of the Spotted Poland China is 50% white with black spots.

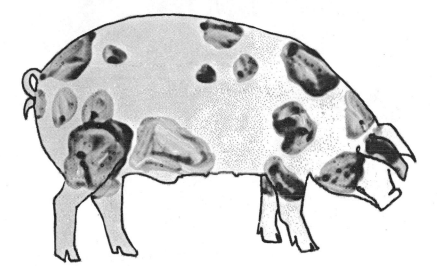

Spotted Poland China

The Tamsworth Breed

The Tamsworth breed of Tamsworth, England is one of the so-called bacon-type hogs. It is one of the oldest and probably purest of all breeds of hogs. The Tamsworth has become popular in the United States only in recent years. With lard becoming an unwanted item, more interest has been shown in the bacon types, especially in cross-breeding programs.

The color of the Tamsworth is red, varying from light to dark. They are long legged, with long, smooth sides and strong backs. The head is long and narrow with large, erect ears. The Tamsworth produces bacon of the finest quality. The sows are very prolific and excellent mothers. The pigs are excellent foragers. Mature boars in show condition weigh from 700 to 900 pounds, and mature sows from 550 to 700 pounds. They are heavy for their size.

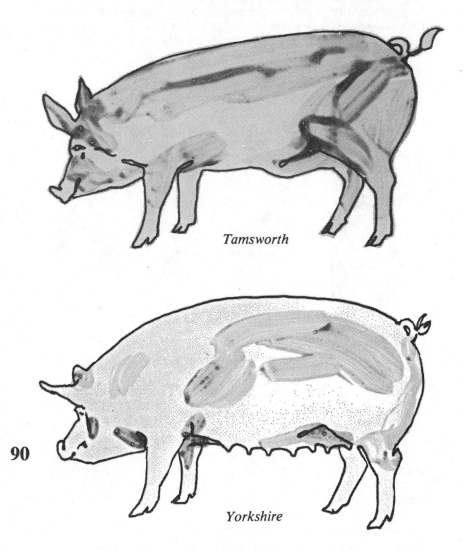

Tamsworth

Yorkshire

The Yorkshire Breed

The Yorkshire breed, like the Tamsworth, is a bacon-type imported from England. The Yorkshire is white in color and smooth, and has a long, deep body. The loins are large, but the hams sometimes lack depth. The Yorkshire sows are extremely fine mothers. They raise large litters of pigs and are very good milkers.

Cross-breeding

In recent years there has been a big change in the desired type of hogs raised for market. To achieve some of the goals, a big cross-breeding program has been carried on. Some crossbreds have performed so well they are almost considered to be a breed unto themselves. Cross-breeding will undoubtedly continue as hog producers seek to meet the changing demands of consumers.

No one breed is greatly superior to the others in its ability to produce meat, to grow rapidly, or to produce large litters. A small acreage farmer can develop a herd of good meat hogs from any one of these breeds.

Glossary

Additive gene
The genes that produce traits or characteristics by adding block upon block through heritability.

Artificial insemination
A mechanical means of impregnating a female with male sperm cells.

Bacon-type hog
A type of hog that was developed to produce lean meat with very little fat.

Boar
Male hog that is used for breeding.

Calf
The young of the cow, normally considered to be less than one year old.

Calf drop
That period of time when cows give birth to their offspring.

Chromosomes
Basophilic-containing cells that control the traits and/or characteristics of offspring.

Colostrum
The first milk that is given by the mother after the young is born.

Concentrates
Feeds that are high in protein.

Confinement housing
A type of housing where animals are cared for from birth to marketing under completely controlled conditions.

Conformation
The proportionate shape of an animal as compared to an ideal model.

92   **Creep feeding**
Feeding of grain or high protein feed to young animals while they are still nursing.

Cross-breeding
Breeding animals of one standard breed to those of a different standard breed, such as using a Hereford bull with Angus cows.

Cull
An inferior animal in a herd that is a nonproducer or a low producer.

Cutting chute
A chute with a gate arrangement that facilitates the separation of animals into groups.

Dressing percentage
The amount of usable meat that is obtained from a live animal.
Ewe
A female sheep.
Farrow box or crate
An enclosure used to confine a sow during farrowing and early nursing of her young.
Farrowing
The birthing of pigs by a sow.
Feeders
Animals that have been fed on grass and rough forage and are ready for transfer to a feed lot for finishing.
Feeding out
The finishing of animals confined in a fattening pen or lot.
Feed lot
An area where animals are confined while they are fed fattening rations.
Finishing
Another term used for the final fattening period of animals.
Finishing ration
A ration high in grains and protein fed to animals during the final fattening period before slaughter.
Flushing
Feeding the female a rich ration a few days prior to breeding.
Forages
Grasses and fodder when used for grazing.
Foundation hogs
The breeding animals used to establish a herd of hogs.
Frost-cured grass
Grass that remains after the growing season that has been killed by frost or freezing weather.
Genes
An element of the germ plasm that controls the transmission of hereditary character.
Genetics
The biology that deals with heredity and its variations.

Gestation period
The period of time that the female carries her young during pregnancy.
Gilt
A young female hog.
Grease wool
The natural wool as it comes from the sheep before being cleaned.
Head gate
A special gate that restrains an animal by clamping its head in a fixed position.

Heritability
Traits that are passed from parents to their offspring.
Hog
A domestic swine, usually applied to an animal weighing more than 130 pounds.
Hybrid vigor
A marked vigor or capacity for growth often shown by crossbred animals.
Inbreeding
The breeding of closely related animals, such as mother to son, father to daughter or sister to brother.
Meat-type hog
A type of hog bred to produce full loins, hams and lean meat.
Mutton breed
A breed of sheep raised primarily for meat; wool is secondary.
Outbreeding
The breeding of unrelated animals.
Outcrossed
The use of two line bred animals with two completely different pedigrees.
Parturition
The process of giving birth to offspring.
Pig
A young swine, usually considered to weigh less than 130 pounds.
Pin bones
The two small knobby bones on either side of the base of a cow's tail.
Polled breed
A breed of cattle that does not have horns.
Progeny test
The testing of the offspring of a male animal to determine if they possess desired characteristics.
Silage
Green fodder that has undergone anaerobic acid fermentation in a silo.

Sow
An adult female swine.
Vulva
The opening between the projecting parts of the female genital organs.
Weaning
The process of separating an offspring from its mother so it can no longer nurse.
Yearling
An animal that has reached its first birthday, but not its second.

COUNTRY HOME & SMALL FARM GUIDES

Planning A Country Place
Evaluating vacant land, inspecting the country home, planning a farmstead, choosing tractors & tools, building fences & barns.

The Pleasure Horse
How to select, buy, house, feed and care for a family riding horse. Includes tack, training, habits and breeds.

Cattle, Sheep & Hogs
How to purchase, house, feed and care for beef cattle, sheep or hogs on a few acres.

Goats, Rabbits & Chickens
How to purchase, house, feed and care for goats, rabbits or chickens on a few acres.

Orchard Handbook
Complete growing and care instructions for apples, peaches, nectarines, pears, plums, apricots, cherries, dwarf fruit trees, propagation and beekeeping on a few acres.

Vegetable Farming
How to grow 25 vegetables as small acreage field crops to feed your family and sell to local markets. Covers soils, fertilization, seeding, cultivation, harvesting and marketing.

Nuts, Berries & Grapes
Complete growing and care instructions for walnuts, pecans, chestnuts, almonds, blackberries, strawberries, blueberries and grapes.

Crops On a Few Acres
Seedbed preparation, planting, cultivation, weed & insect control and harvesting instruction for corn, wheat, oats, peanuts, soybeans, sorghums, pasture and forage crops, cotton and tobacco.